T0194684

An Analysis of

Gayatri Chakravorty Spivak's

Can the Subaltern Speak?

Graham K. Riach

Published by Macat International Ltd
24:13 Coda Centre, 189 Munster Road, London SW6 6AW.

Distributed exclusively by Routledge
2 Park Square, Milton Park, Abingdon, Oxon OX14 4RN
711 Third Avenue, New York, NY 10017, USA

Routledge is an imprint of the Taylor & Francis Group, an informa business

Copyright © 2017 by Macat International Ltd
Macat International has asserted its right under the Copyright, Designs and Patents Act
1988 to be identified as the copyright holder of this work.

The print publication is protected by copyright. Prior to any prohibited reproduction, storage in
a retrieval system, distribution or transmission in any form or by any means, electronic, mechanical, recording or otherwise, permission should be obtained from the publisher or where
applicable a license permitting restricted copying in the United Kingdom should be obtained
from the Copyright Licensing Agency Ltd, Barnard's Inn, 86 Fetter Lane, London EC4A 1EN, UK.

The ePublication is protected by copyright and must not be copied, reproduced, transferred,
distributed, leased, licensed or publicly performed or used in any way except as specifically
permitted in writing by the publishers, as allowed under the terms and conditions under which
it was purchased, or as strictly permitted by applicable copyright law. Any unauthorised distribution or use of this text may be a direct infringement of the authors and the publishers' rights
and those responsible may be liable in law accordingly.

www.macat.com
info@macat.com

Cataloguing in Publication Data
A catalogue record for this book is available from the British Library.
Library of Congress Cataloguing-in-Publication Data is available upon request.
Cover illustration: Etienne Gilfillan

ISBN 978-1-912302-89-5 (hardback)
ISBN 978-1-912127-50-4 (paperback)
ISBN 978-1-912281-77-0 (e-book)

Notice
The information in this book is designed to orientate readers of the work under analysis,
to elucidate and contextualise its key ideas and themes, and to aid in the development
of critical thinking skills. It is not meant to be used, nor should it be used, as a
substitute for original thinking or in place of original writing or research. References and
notes are provided for informational purposes and their presence does not constitute
endorsement of the information or opinions therein. This book is presented solely for
educational purposes. It is sold on the understanding that the publisher is not engaged
to provide any scholarly advice. The publisher has made every effort to ensure that
this book is accurate and up-to-date, but makes no warranties or representations with
regard to the completeness or reliability of the information it contains. The information
and the opinions provided herein are not guaranteed or warranted to produce particular
results and may not be suitable for students of every ability. The publisher shall not be
liable for any loss, damage or disruption arising from any errors or omissions, or from
the use of this book, including, but not limited to, special, incidental, consequential or
other damages caused, or alleged to have been caused, directly or indirectly, by the
information contained within.

CONTENTS

THE MACAT LIBRARY

The Macat Library is a series of unique academic explorations of seminal works in the humanities and social sciences – books and papers that have had a significant and widely recognised impact on their disciplines. It has been created to serve as much more than just a summary of what lies between the covers of a great book. It illuminates and explores the influences on, ideas of, and impact of that book. Our goal is to offer a learning resource that encourages critical thinking and fosters a better, deeper understanding of important ideas.

Each publication is divided into three Sections: Influences, Ideas, and Impact. Each Section has four Modules. These explore every important facet of the work, and the responses to it.

This Section-Module structure makes a Macat Library book easy to use, but it has another important feature. Because each Macat book is written to the same format, it is possible (and encouraged!) to cross-reference multiple Macat books along the same lines of inquiry or research. This allows the reader to open up interesting interdisciplinary pathways.

To further aid your reading, lists of glossary terms and people mentioned are included at the end of this book (these are indicated by an asterisk [*] throughout) – as well as a list of works cited.

Macat has worked with the University of Cambridge to identify the elements of critical thinking and understand the ways in which six different skills combine to enable effective thinking.
Three allow us to fully understand a problem; three more give us the tools to solve it. Together, these six skills make up the **PACIER** model of critical thinking. They are:

ANALYSIS – understanding how an argument is built
EVALUATION – exploring the strengths and weaknesses of an argument
INTERPRETATION – understanding issues of meaning

CREATIVE THINKING – coming up with new ideas and fresh connections
PROBLEM-SOLVING – producing strong solutions
REASONING – creating strong arguments

To find out more, visit **WWW.MACAT.COM.**

CRITICAL THINKING AND "CAN THE SUBALTERN SPEAK?"

Primary critical thinking skill: INTERPRETATION
Secondary critical thinking skill: REASONING

A key theme of Gayatri Spivak's work is agency: the ability of the individual to make their own decisions. While Spivak's main aim is to consider ways in which "subalterns" – her term for the indigenous dispossessed in colonial societies – were able to achieve agency, this paper concentrates specifically on describing the ways in which western scholars inadvertently reproduce hegemonic structures in their work.

Spivak is herself a scholar, and she remains acutely aware of the difficulty and dangers of presuming to "speak" for the subalterns she writes about. As such, her work can be seen as predominantly a delicate exercise in the critical thinking skill of interpretation; she looks in detail at issues of meaning, specifically at the real meaning of the available evidence, and her paper is an attempt not only to highlight problems of definition, but to clarify them.

What makes this one of the key works of interpretation in the Macat library is, of course, the underlying significance of this work. Interpretation, in this case, is a matter of the difference between allowing subalterns to speak for themselves, and of imposing a mode of "speaking" on them that – however well-intentioned – can be as damaging in the postcolonial world as the agency-stifling political structures of the colonial world itself. By clearing away the detritus of scholarly attempts at interpretation, Spivak takes a stand against a specifically intellectual form of oppression and marginalization.

ABOUT THE AUTHOR OF THE ORIGINAL WORK

Gayatri Chakravorty Spivak is a leading figure in postcolonial studies, the academic field that examines the impact of colonial control on former colonies. She was born in India in 1942, five years before the country gained its independence from Britain, and first studied in India before completing graduate degrees in Britain and the United States. For a number of years, she has been a faculty member at the prestigious Columbia University in New York City. Spivak's work has been highly influential, but she has been criticized for her extremely theoretical, dense texts. She is also an activist, teaching and helping set up schools among the world's poorest communities.

ABOUT THE AUTHOR OF THE ANALYSIS

Dr Graham Riach holds a PhD from Emmanuel College, Cambridge, on contemporary South African literature. A specialist in postcolonial literature, he currently teaches at the University of Oxford.

ABOUT MACAT

GREAT WORKS FOR CRITICAL THINKING

Macat is focused on making the ideas of the world's great thinkers accessible and comprehensible to everybody, everywhere, in ways that promote the development of enhanced critical thinking skills.

It works with leading academics from the world's top universities to produce new analyses that focus on the ideas and the impact of the most influential works ever written across a wide variety of academic disciplines. Each of the works that sit at the heart of its growing library is an enduring example of great thinking. But by setting them in context – and looking at the influences that shaped their authors, as well as the responses they provoked – Macat encourages readers to look at these classics and game-changers with fresh eyes. Readers learn to think, engage and challenge their ideas, rather than simply accepting them.

'Macat offers an amazing first-of-its-kind tool for interdisciplinary learning and research. Its focus on works that transformed their disciplines and its rigorous approach, drawing on the world's leading experts and educational institutions, opens up a world-class education to anyone.'

Andreas Schleicher
Director for Education and Skills, Organisation for Economic
Co-operation and Development

'Macat is taking on some of the major challenges in university education … They have drawn together a strong team of active academics who are producing teaching materials that are novel in the breadth of their approach.'

Prof Lord Broers,
former Vice-Chancellor of the University of Cambridge

'The Macat vision is exceptionally exciting. It focuses upon new modes of learning which analyse and explain seminal texts which have profoundly influenced world thinking and so social and economic development. It promotes the kind of critical thinking which is essential for any society and economy. This is the learning of the future.'

Rt Hon Charles Clarke, former UK Secretary of State for Education

'The Macat analyses provide immediate access to the critical conversation surrounding the books that have shaped their respective discipline, which will make them an invaluable resource to all of those, students and teachers, working in the field.'

Professor William Tronzo, University of California at San Diego

WAYS IN TO THE TEXT

KEY POINTS

- Gayatri Chakravorty Spivak was born in Calcutta in 1942, and was educated in both India and America. Her experience in these two countries informed her later work

- In her pioneering essay, "Can the Subaltern Speak?" (1988), Spivak argues that the world's poorest people have no voice in society. She claims that the local elite—officials, educators, religious leaders—and Western scholars can never faithfully speak* for them.

- "Can the Subaltern Speak?" is notable for its bold criticism of Western scholars who study the poor and excluded, and its concern for gender* in postcolonial* studies (inquiry into the various effects and legacies of colonialism,* particularly through the study of language and culture).

Who Is Gayatri Chakravorty Spivak?

Gayatri Chakravorty Spivak, author of the essay "Can the Subaltern Speak?" (1988), was born in Kolkata (formerly Calcutta) on February 24, 1942, five years before India gained its independence from Britain. This early experience in India may have shaped her later interest in subalterns*—the poorest, most excluded members of society.

Spivak is widely recognized as one of the most important postcolonial intellectuals—scholars examining the effects of foreign domination on the former colonies of European nations such as Britain and France. She has done pioneering work in subaltern studies,* an area of research concerned with the history of the world's very poorest—those with no education or jobs, and no means to get them.

Spivak graduated, before her 18th birthday, from the University of Calcutta in 1959 with a first-class honors degree in English and gold medals in English and Bengali literature. She left India for the United States in 1959 and earned a Master's degree at Cornell University in the American state of New York. She completed a year's fellowship at Girton College at Britain's Cambridge University, then returned to America to complete a PhD at Cornell, supervised by the deconstructionist* philosopher Paul de Man.* Deconstructionism seeks to "deconstruct" texts through methods such as the identification of the ideological biases—gender, racial, economic, political, cultural—that they carry. After her PhD, she taught at several American universities, and became a translator and postcolonial theorist (that is, she produced theories to try to better understand things observed in the world—in her case, the powerlessness of the very poor). She is now a professor at Columbia University in New York City, in the Department of English and Comparative Literature.

In parallel with her academic career, Spivak is also a political activist and educator. Theory and practice go hand in hand in her work. She has set up schools in the Indian region of West Bengal, and has taught in Algeria and China, among other places. While academics often spend most of their careers in the comfort of their university campuses, her decision to spend time in the field, in practical work with the poor, provides a different model of how to conduct an academic career.

What Does "Can the Subaltern Speak?" Say?

The title of Spivak's essay "Can the Subaltern Speak?" is somewhat misleading. While it certainly explores whether subalterns can speak, it is more interested in whether they can be *heard*. Spivak argues that there are a number of factors preventing this. The most important is that more powerful people—academics, religious leaders, or people who are otherwise privileged in society—always speak for them. When they do this, the elite rob subalterns of their own voice. If subalterns could both speak and have a forum in which to be heard (the "speak" of the essay's title), Spivak hopes these people would achieve an effective political voice.

Spivak combines ideas from Marxism* (here an approach critical of capitalist economic exploitation), feminism* (promotion of equality between the sexes), and deconstruction. These specialties help her make an argument about the oppression caused by differences in power, gender, and access to knowledge.

She discusses how scholarship, and particularly Western scholarship, always misrepresents so-called "Third World"* peoples (those from the developing countries), and shows why subaltern women are doubly marginalized (first as the colonized, then again as women). Spivak focuses on what she calls "epistemic violence"*[1]—violence inflicted through thought, speech, and writing, rather than actual physical harm. For Spivak, a good example of epistemic violence is when accounts of history leave out subalterns. When oppressed peoples are not allowed to speak for themselves, or to have their contributions recognized, they are in effect erased from their place in the world. This is especially common for subaltern women. In Spivak's words: "If, in the context of colonial production, the subaltern has no history and cannot speak, the subaltern as female is even more deeply in shadow."[2] For Spivak, women are silenced by both colonialism and patriarchy* (broadly, a system of societal organization in which men hold most or all positions of power).

Spivak concludes that "the subaltern cannot speak."[3] This is because they are always spoken *for* by those in positions of power, and are never able to represent themselves. Further, if they do speak, they are not heard. Spivak understands speaking as a transaction between a listener and a speaker, writing: "When you say cannot speak, it means that if speaking involves speaking and listening, this possibility of response, responsibility, does not exist in the subaltern's sphere."[4] A poor peasant can say: "No matter how hard I work, my family does not have enough to eat." But will this be heard in a way that can begin to effect change? For speech to be successful, it must transmit its message. For Spivak, subaltern speech does not achieve this.

Spivak's essay is one of the standard texts of postcolonial studies. It has been widely republished in collections of her work. It is translated into many languages, including Spanish, German, Chinese, and Hebrew, and is rarely absent from postcolonial studies readers. "Can the Subaltern Speak?" is unique in its integration of deconstructionist and feminist thought into a critique of the social, cultural, and political impact of colonialism—the occupation and exploitation of one territory or nation by another.

Why Does "Can the Subaltern Speak?" Matter?

The impact of the essay has been profound. It sparked furious debate in the academic community about how intellectuals play a role in silencing subaltern voices. By speaking for subalterns, Spivak suggests, even well-meaning academics can do harm. Spivak's ideas have been influential for postcolonial studies and literary criticism. They have also been taken up in other disciplines, such as history, anthropology (the study of human beings, commonly with an emphasis on culture and society), archaeology (the study of the traces of historical human activity), and cultural studies. Its ideas are also used in the work of political activists.

Her essay offers a perspective on many key postcolonial concerns:

- The dangers of believing that Western thinking can be used in non-Western contexts without causing problems.
- The ethical issues that arise when representing and speaking for others.
- How to restore indigenous (so-called "native") cultures that were systematically pushed down under colonialism.
- How history might be told from the point of view of the colonized, rather than the colonizer.
- The relationship between colonialism and other systems of oppression, including patriarchy and, to her mind, capitalism* (a social and economic system in which trade and industry are exercised for the sake of private profit).

Spivak's essay asks readers to consider the beliefs they bring to their dealings with other cultures, and to acknowledge that these beliefs can lead to mistakes in understanding. The essay encourages readers to question their own thinking, and to be aware that it is never neutral; what we take to be common sense is often informed by our cultural background, and Spivak forces us to remain aware of this when dealing with other cultures.

On a more immediate level, Spivak's text is a call to arms, and one that keeps its urgency today. While the argument is abstract, there is a solid practical core, as she makes clear in an interview, insisting that it is our duty to "work for the bloody subaltern ... against subalternity."[5] In other words, it is not enough just to let subalterns speak from their subaltern position; rather, we have to work to rethink structures of power—colonialism, law, academia, government, economics, patriarchy—and so end the exclusion of some members of society that creates subalterns in the first place.

NOTES

1   Gayatri Chakravorty Spivak, "Can the Subaltern Speak?," in *Marxism and the Interpretation of Culture* (Basingstoke: Macmillan Education, 1988), 280.

2   Spivak, "Can the Subaltern Speak?," 287.

3   Spivak, "Can the Subaltern Speak?," 308.

4   Gayatri Chakravorty Spivak and Leon de Kock, "Interview with Gayatri Chakravorty Spivak: New Nation Writers Conference in South Africa," *ARIEL: A Review of International English Literature* 23, no. 3 (1992): 46.

5   Spivak and de Kock, "Interview," 46.

SECTION 1
INFLUENCES

THE AUTHOR AND THE HISTORICAL CONTEXT

KEY POINTS

- "Can the Subaltern Speak?" is one of the founding texts of postcolonial* studies (the study of the various effects and legacies of colonialism,* commonly with a focus on culture and language), and remains highly influential.

- Spivak's early education by subaltern* women—women of conspicuously low social status—shaped her ideas about societal hierarchies and the limits on the decision making and actions of subaltern people.

- Spivak's work was deeply influenced by the decolonization of India in 1947, giving her experience of colonial and postcolonial life that stayed with her.

Why Read This Text?

In her 1988 essay "Can the Subaltern Speak?" Gayatri Chakravorty Spivak, a professor at Columbia University, examines the situation of subalterns—people who are kept in an inferior position in society due to their class, caste, age, gender, or other reason. Whether due to colonialism (the policy and practice of occupation and exploitation by one nation of another), patriarchy* (a system in which male authority is paramount), or other systems, such people are systematically denied the opportunity to participate in public debate, and to represent themselves in the political system, the media, the educational system, and so on. Spivak focuses on self-representation in political, legal, and academic contexts, being interested in how, by speaking* for themselves, subalterns might avoid being misrepresented by others.

> **❝** I was born in British India. When I was going to school, the system of education had not yet started its process of systematic decolonization. My generation at college was among the first generations to really kind of feel that they were in independent India. **❞**
>
> Gayatri Chakravorty Spivak and Leon de Kock, "Interview with Gayatri Chakravorty Spivak"

According to Spivak, Western inquiries into the societies of developing nations come with ideological biases (that is, the scholars cannot be neutral, and always look at things from their own point of view); this, in turn, silences indigenous—local or "native"—viewpoints. To make this argument, Spivak brings together a unique combination of Marxist,* poststructuralist,* and feminist* theories ("Marxism" refers to the methods and theories of the political philosopher Karl Marx,* according to whom economic factors are the principal drivers of history; "poststructuralism" refers to a philosophical approach that questions the structures through which knowledge is produced, destabilizing claims to universal truth; "feminist" refers to the various intellectual and political currents associated with the struggle for equality between the sexes). Spivak examines examples of how Western intellectuals portray subalterns, showing why such approaches are insufficient for describing non-Western societies; further, she investigates what possibilities subaltern women have for speaking and being heard.

"Can the Subaltern Speak?" is a core text of postcolonial studies, and has gained international recognition. It has been republished widely, is regularly taught in universities, and continues to generate heated debate. Spivak's arguments have been used, extended, and transformed by a range of literary scholars, feminists, historians, and political activists. Although written in the 1980s, the text's criticism of cultural oppression continues to resonate today.

Author's Life

Spivak's father was a doctor who died when Spivak was only 13, and her mother was "married at fourteen and with children coming at ... fifteen and twenty-three," yet she still "studied in private and obtained her MA in Bengali literature from Calcutta University in 1937."[1] She calls her family background "solidly metropolitan middle class."[2] Her early schooling took place at a missionary school in Calcutta, where she was taught by converts to Christianity from a much lower social standing than her own. Critic Stephen Morton has suggested that this early experience of being taught by women who overcame their marginalized position has "continued to mark the trajectory of Spivak's work,"[3] by sensitizing her to the possible agency of subalterns—the ways they find to recognize, express, and act on their desires and decisions.

Spivak completed her undergraduate studies in English at the University of Calcutta's Presidency College in 1959. She was immersed there in the canon* (key works) of English literature, understood as the literature of Great Britain. She was also exposed to left-wing political activism. These two influences were central to shaping her later work, in which she critiqued works such as the Victorian novelist Charlotte Brontë's* *Jane Eyre*,* for their implicit support of colonial ideology* (a system of beliefs forming a particular world view).

After a Master's degree at Cornell University, and a one-year fellowship at Cambridge University's Girton College, she returned to Cornell to complete a doctoral degree under the supervision of the Belgian literary theorist Paul de Man.* His influence on her work is most immediately visible in her use of deconstructionist* approaches, which question absolute truths, and which pick apart the contradictions of language in literature and philosophy.

While teaching at various American institutions, Spivak published "Can the Subaltern Speak?" first in the journal *Wedge* (1985), and then in its extended and best-known form in the collection *Marxism and the Interpretation of Culture* (1988).

She took up a post at Columbia University in 1992, later becoming the director of the Center for Comparative Literature and Society, and in 2007 was named University Professor, which is the highest faculty rank at Columbia.

In 2012, Spivak received the Kyoto Prize in Arts and Philosophy, and in 2013 she was given the highly prestigious Padma Bhushan* civic award by the Indian government. She is also known as a philanthropist, having set up the Pares Chandra Chakravorty Memorial Literacy Project, a nonprofit organization that provides education in some of the world's poorest regions. In other words, her academic work is complemented by a more hands-on approach to bettering the lives of subalterns.

Author's Background

The most important historical factor that influenced Spivak's work was probably the decolonization of India, which picked up speed in the late 1800s, eventually leading to independence in 1947. According to one scholar, it was "this political context in pre-independence Calcutta that shaped Spivak's earliest childhood experience."[4] Spivak was born in 1942, into a climate of civil unrest over the Bengal Famine*—a disaster in which some millions died—and while anti-colonial nationalist movements were growing.

In the decades that followed independence, the continuing effects of colonization on India became more apparent. These included ongoing ethnic and religious rivalries, the legacy of institutional violence in the systems of law and government, the continued use of the English university curriculum, and the continuing oppression of minority groups. Spivak was acutely aware of the wounds that colonialism had inflicted on Indian society, and that these had not been healed by the seeming liberation from oppression that came with becoming an independent nation. Further, her experience of this as a relatively privileged middle-class Hindu* woman made her sensitive to the more subtle differences between formerly colonized individuals. (Hinduism is the largest religion in the Indian subcontinent.) Spivak made it her life's work to speak back to systems of oppression, by adapting the philosophical and critical tools she had learned to undermine the cultural imperialism* of the West*—that is, the spread of Western values and cultural norms as a means to cement Western political and economic dominance.

NOTES

1   Gayatri Chakravorty Spivak, "Translation as Culture," in *In Translation: Reflections, Refractions, Transformations*, ed. Paul St-Pierre and Prafulla C. Kar (Amsterdam: John Benjamins, 2007), 272.

2   Gayatri Chakravorty Spivak, *The Postcolonial Critic: Interviews, Strategies, Dialogues*, ed. Sarah Harasym (London: Routledge, 1990), 165.

3   Stephen Morton, *Gayatri Spivak: Ethics, Subalternity and the Critique of Postcolonial Reason* (Cambridge: Polity, 2007), 4.

4   Morton, *Gayatri Spivak: Ethics*, 4.

ACADEMIC CONTEXT

KEY POINTS

- Spivak was a pioneer of the postcolonial* approach in the analysis of literature from former colonies, rejecting the dominant approach that saw the literature of colonizing countries as both superior and uninfluenced by colonialism.*

- Spivak's work builds on that of anti-colonial and postcolonial theorists such as the poet and politician Aimé Césaire* and the social philosopher and psychiatrist Frantz Fanon,* both from Martinique, and the Indian liberation leader Mohandas Karamchand Gandhi.*

- Spivak was strongly influenced by several other scholars, notably the Palestinian American scholar Edward Said,* a founder of the field of postcolonial studies.

The Work in its Context

Gayatri Chakravorty Spivak's essay "Can the Subaltern Speak?" is an interdisciplinary work (a work drawing on the aims and methods of different academic disciplines), combining philosophy and history with Marxist* and feminist* approaches; according to Marxist analysis, economics—notably the struggle between different social classes—are the principal driver of history; the feminist approach draws on theoretical currents that acknowledge the inequality between the sexes. It is, then, appropriate that the work is considered a standard text in the broad field of postcolonial studies, which brings together scholars from a number of disciplines, all sharing a critical interest in the cultural and material effects of colonialism and its aftermath. They seek, for example, to:

> ❝ Spivak's critical negotiation of Marxism and deconstruction is perhaps better understood if it is situated within a broader intellectual history of decolonization... ❞
>
> Stephen Morton, *Gayatri Spivak: Ethics, Subalternity and the Critique of Postcolonial Reason*, citing Robert J. C. Young, *Postcolonialism: An Historical Introduction*

- offer revisionist* readings (that is, comprehensive reevaluations) of Western historical accounts
- show the lasting influence of the colonial past on the present
- make readers aware of the blind spots in their cultural perspective
- denounce ongoing imperialism* in the present ("imperialism" refers to the various cultural, economic, and social forms of "empire building" which serve to entrench the interests of dominant societies or nations).

Spivak was one of the pioneers of using postcolonial approaches to analyze literary texts. Prior to her work, the literature from nations newly independent of their colonial "masters" was widely considered the literature of the former ruling country and its former colonies; the literature of Britain's numerous former colonies was termed "Commonwealth Literature,"* for example. This is a problematic classification, as it gives a Eurocentric* view of English literary studies: it upholds a Center–Periphery model* of culture, in which the culture of the colonizing country is taken to be dominant and superior (in this case, a conception of the world in which Europe is taken to be the most important place, and everything else exists only in relation to it). "Commonwealth Literature" also ignored that British literature was part of the Commonwealth, and further lacked a strong critical approach. Postcolonial Literature, a field launched in part by "Can the Subaltern Speak?," might be thought

a combination of Commonwealth Literature and "critical theory"*
(an analytical approach seeking to uncover and critique the hidden
social and cultural messages of cultural production), lending it a
strong theoretical framework.

Overview of the Field

Spivak's work in postcolonial studies was indebted to a number
of thinkers. The main wave of anti-colonial thought took place in
the 1950s and 1960s. It included theorists such as Aimé Césaire,
whose essay *Discourse on Colonialism* (1955) criticized racist colonial
narratives of civilization and progress, and his fellow Martiniquais,
the psychiatrist and theorist Frantz Fanon, whose books *Black Skin,
White Masks* (1952) and *The Wretched of the Earth* (1961) explored
the psychological damage caused by forcing Western values on
indigenous peoples.

More geographically immediate to Spivak was the Indian
liberation leader Mohandas Karamchand Gandhi, whose 1909
anti-colonial pamphlet *Hind Swaraj* ("Indian Home Rule") offered
an angry criticism of European arrogance, condemning Western
modernity* (those things that define modern Western culture)
and laying out a program of nonviolent resistance to English rule.
Gandhi specifically did not just want "English rule without the
Englishman"[1]—the maintenance of English societal structures by
Indian people; he wanted, rather, a completely new model of society
that rejected European modernity in its entirety.

Spivak has translated Césaire, has provided the introduction to
a film on Fanon and spoken on his work, and has quoted Gandhi's
"Indian Home Rule" favorably when discussing violence in
revolutionary movements.[2] These three thinkers not only provided
a substantial part of the framework behind the emerging field of
postcolonial studies in the 1980s; they were also theorists with
whom Spivak engaged directly in her academic writing.

Academic Influences

While Spivak has not closely allied herself with any single intellectual school of thought, her immediate academic influences can be split into three main groups:

- The Subaltern Studies Group* (a group of scholars focusing on South Asia).
- Poststructuralist* philosophy, most notably that of the French theorist Jacques Derrida* and the Belgian thinker Paul de Man.*
- Edward Said (a figure considered foundational in the field of postcolonialist studies).

The Subaltern Studies Group is led by the historian Ranajit Guha,* and initially included the scholar of history and political science Partha Chatterjee* and others. This group set out to write a history "from below" of the development of nationalist consciousness in India—that is, shifting the focus of the historical study from the elite to a "politics of the people."[3] In so doing, their work attempts to give the dispossessed in India (India's poor and excluded) a voice. Spivak has had a long association with this group. While she is largely supportive of their work, she voices methodological differences from them in "Can the Subaltern Speak?"

The second major influence on Spivak's work is poststructuralist philosophy. This movement contains various thinkers—Derrida, the French social historian and philosopher Michel Foucault,* the gender theorist Judith Butler,* and others—who were grouped together when their work was received in English-speaking universities from the 1960s. Common to most of them is an interest in exposing the metaphysical* assumptions—that is, the first principles informing our thinking—and our interpretation of language. From the 1960s to the 1980s these approaches were popular with the so-called Yale school of deconstruction,* spearheaded by Paul de Man, Spivak's doctoral supervisor. The influence of poststructuralism on Spivak is visible both in her theoretical approach, which seeks to break down established certainties, and in her writing style that is often difficult to understand.

A third important influence on Spivak's work comes from the Palestinian American thinker Edward Said, whose work *Orientalism* (1978) played a key role in establishing the field of postcolonial studies[4] (according to the British postcolonialist theorist Robert Young,* colonial discourse analysis* was "initiated as an academic subdiscipline within literary and cultural theory" by this work).[5] Said set out to demonstrate that Western representations of the Orient*—here the Middle East and Far East— always misrepresent the societies they describe, as the European research approaches they use bring with them various false ideas and prejudices. These ways of looking at the Orient are not neutral, and have been used to enforce colonial rule, and to prop up a self-flattering portrayal of an enlightened, clean, productive West* in contrast to a primitive, dirty, passive Orient. This is important to Spivak's essay, as it shows how oppression can be carried out through scholarly or cultural means, as much as through brute force—an argument she develops.

Furthermore, and crucially to understanding "Can the Subaltern Speak?," Said argues that Western ways of discussing the Orient silenced the voices of those who lived there, stripping them of the power of representing themselves. Spivak's approach adopts a similar position. But while Said portrays the roles of the colonizer and the colonized as relatively fixed, Spivak shows colonial identities to be more shifting and unsteady.

NOTES

1   Mohandas Karamchand Gandhi, *Hind Swaraj or Indian Home Rule* [1909] (Ahmedabad: Navajivan, 1938), 30.

2   Gayatri Chakravorty Spivak and Bulan Lahiri, "In Conversation: Speaking to Spivak," *The Hindu*, February 5, 2011, accessed November 26, 2015, http://www.thehindu.com/books/in-conversation-speaking-to-spivak/article1159208.ece.

3   Ranajit Guha, *A Subaltern Studies Reader, 1986–1995* (New Delhi: Oxford University Press, 1997), xiv.

4   Edward Saïd, *Orientalism* (New York: Pantheon, 1978).

5   Robert J. C. Young, *Colonial Desire: Hybridity in Theory, Culture and Race* (London: Routledge, 1995), 159.

MODULE 3
THE PROBLEM

KEY POINTS

- "Can the Subaltern Speak?" is an essay concerning the representations of those denied a voice on account of their low social status, and how the independent agency of these "subalterns"* (their ability to make their own decisions) is suppressed by the powerful in society.

- While Spivak contributes to the work of historians of colonialism* and of the Subaltern Studies Group,* she also doubts aspects of the methods they use in their work.

- Spivak questions why some historians spoke of subalterns as if they acted as a homogeneous (internally alike) group rather than as distinct individuals with their own interests.

Core Question

Although her examples are largely taken from India, the themes Gayatri Chakravorty Spivak takes up in "Can the Subaltern Speak?" have global importance.

Written after Indian independence* from Britain, this essay is an attack on the continuing impact of colonialism. Spivak's focus is on how systems of knowledge—particularly Western scholarly work— lead to what she calls "epistemic violence":* violence inflicted through discourse.* "Discourse" refers to the systems of language and assumptions used to discuss and think about specific things; in this context, it signifies the words that support a particular ideology,* or that are used to justify political and military domination. If the media or politicians portray a group as a threat (consider the ways

> 66 This question of representation, self-representation, representing others, is a problem. 99
>
> Gayatri Chakravorty Spivak, *The Post-colonial Critic*

that Muslims are often represented, for example), this begins by damaging their reputation, and can then be used to justify the use of force against them.

The essay's central concern is how representing subalterns (with "representing" here meaning when scholars, politicians and lawyers talk about them, or in their place), and so speaking* on their behalf, effectively silences their own voices. The essay has a clear political purpose: to expose how seemingly neutral systems of representation are in fact slanted towards the privileged in society. If subalterns cannot speak and be heard, Spivak questions whether there is an ethically sound way for the privileged to speak *for* them.

Spivak's essay was an early contribution to a new wave of critiques about the aftereffects of colonialism. Many European colonies, among them India, Ghana, and the Republic of the Congo, gained their independence between the 1940s and the 1970s. Historians, such as the academics of the Subaltern Studies Group, and theorists, such as Edward Said* and Spivak, started to consider what colonialism had done to former colonies. "Can the Subaltern Speak?" is a furious response to the ideological power that the West* continues to hold over the countries it once ruled—the way the West continues to impose its ways of thinking.

The Participants

The essay appeared in an intellectual climate in which the experiences of postcolonial nations were gaining increasing attention from a new generation of thinkers. Postcolonialist* critics such as Said and Spivak argued that all Western acts of writing about, or otherwise representing, the developing world were forms of exercising power. Underlying these new approaches were poststructural* frameworks adapted from philosophers such as Michel Foucault* and Jacques Derrida*—theorists who broadly reject the idea that there is an objective reality that exists outside systems of discourse: there are, they argue, only competing claims on truth by people speaking from politically interested positions. For poststructuralist thinkers, what these people say, and how they say it, reflects their interests; together these competing claims construct reality as we experience it.

This "postcolonial turn" in scholarship also affected the practice of history. In the 1980s and 1990s, there was a shift away from the economic and political aspects of imperialism studied by historians and economists such as J. A. Hobson* (author of the classic *Imperialism*, 1902), and John Gallagher* and Ronald Robinson* (authors of the similarly influential *Africa and the Victorians: The Official Mind of Imperialism*, 1961). Scholarship turned to a greater concern for "ideas of culture … discourse … attention to gender* relations and/or to racial imaginings" such as false ideas about racial purity and pollution.[1]

The British imperial historian John M. MacKenzie's* *Propaganda and Empire* (1984) is a good example of this "cultural turn"* in history research, as it uses cultural texts—literature and pamphlets, for example—as historical evidence.[2] It is not that this new generation thought economics and politics to be unimportant; rather, they took that importance for granted, and turned their attention to other matters.

In parallel with the studies of these Western historians, in the 1980s a group of South Asian historians known as the Subaltern Studies Group was revolutionizing the practice of history. These historians used innovative methods, such as searching for subaltern voices in court records, to try to give suppressed communities their due in the historical record. While Spivak was broadly supportive of their project, she felt their methodology did not match their aims; for her, it led to reinforcing some of the power structures they hoped to break down.

The Contemporary Debate

Spivak's essay engages directly with the ideas of poststructural philosophers and the research of the Subaltern Studies Group. Her methods are similar to those of cultural historians in that she reads cultural texts to show how they support colonial ideology—but she also takes issue with aspects of these schools of thought.

She criticizes the French poststructuralists Gilles Deleuze* (a thinker notably concerned with matters of identity) and Michel Foucault for underestimating their roles as academics in maintaining oppressive power structures. This is perhaps surprising, given their reputations as radical left-wing intellectuals who have made similar criticisms of others. She asks whether politics designed to help subjugated groups in the West—the working class, for example—are suitable for subalterns in the former colonies, and doubts whether intellectuals can fairly represent voiceless communities.

The Subaltern Studies Group also comes in for criticism. In Spivak's account, the group's methodology falls short on two main counts. First, they falsely suggest that the subaltern population is all the same. In an attempt to establish knowledge of the subalterns and their consciousness, the group flattens the wide differences among subalterns. In Spivak's words, "the colonized subaltern subject is irretrievably heterogeneous"[3] (that is, it is not internally alike). Spivak is wary of imposing a homogeneous view—"the subaltern perspective," as it were—on what is, in fact, a varied group, feeling that there are many different subaltern voices and positions rather than a single subaltern voice.

Second, by continuing to talk about "subaltern" and "elite" as if they were stable categories, the Subaltern Studies Group unwittingly reproduces the inequalities in society that they seek to undo. The concept "subaltern" can only exist in opposition to that of "elite," and so fails to achieve independence from it.

In sum, Spivak's influences are as often academic opponents

as they are allies. While she borrows from various approaches and fields, each one is subject to an intense process of questioning, even as they are incorporated into her approach.

NOTES

1   Stephen Howe, ed., *The New Imperial Histories Reader* (London; New York: Routledge, 2009), 2.

2   John M. MacKenzie, *Propaganda and Empire: The Manipulation of British Public Opinion, 1880–1960* (Manchester: Manchester University Press, 1984).

3   Gayatri Chakravorty Spivak, "Can the Subaltern Speak?," in *Marxism and the Interpretation of Culture* (Basingstoke: Macmillan Education, 1988), 284.

MODULE 4
THE AUTHOR'S CONTRIBUTION

KEY POINTS

- In "Can the Subaltern Speak?" Gayatri Chakravorty Spivak questions whether current systems of representation, such as politics or law, allow subalterns to speak* and be heard.

- By combining deconstructionist,* Marxist,* and feminist* thought, Spivak offers a unique take on the agency of the subaltern*—that is, their ability to make decisions for themselves.

- Spivak builds on the work of the postcolonialist* thinker Edward Said,* combining his thought with deconstructionist theory adapted from Jacques Derrida*— an approach to the analysis of culture that emphasizes the role of language in the construction of "reality."

Author's Aims

In "Can the Subaltern Speak?" Gayatri Chakravorty Spivak shows some ways in which the legacies of colonialism* continue to affect us. For Spivak, colonialism's oppressive ideology is reproduced through cultural means. She demonstrates that the supposedly disinterested* stance of Western scholarship in fact reproduces the logic of colonialism, in which one party is superior to another. For Spivak, even intellectuals who seem to disapprove of hegemonic* structures of society (roughly, forms of organization that maintain the dominance of certain parties in hierarchical social systems) reproduce those structures themselves by generating knowledge about the oppressed. For her, any "attempt to disclose and know the discourse* of society's Other"*[1]—meaning an attempt to gather information about the oppressed and to represent them in

> **❝** My position is generally a reactive one. I am viewed by Marxists as too codic [abstract], by feminists as too male-identified, by indigenous theorists as too committed to Western Theory. I am uneasily pleased about this. **❞**
>
> Gayatri Chakravorty Spivak, *The Post-colonial Critic*

speech or writing—is to hold some kind of power over them. The capitalized term "Other" in postcolonial studies refers to people from developing nations as perceived by the Western gaze.

Spivak is aware of the irony that her own efforts to understand the subaltern also generate the kind of knowledge of them that she criticizes. As an intellectual, she is far from being a member of "the illiterate peasantry."[2] By presuming to speak for them, she arguably falls foul of her own criticism. Spivak opens her essay by drawing attention to the "precariousness of [her] position."[3] This precariousness, or shakiness, results from the conflict between her aims to show that scholarship cannot represent subalterns ethically, and so should not speak on their behalf, and the act of writing the essay, which speaks out about the injustices done to subalterns, and so offers a kind of political representation for them. She admits that such "gestures" of scholarly self-awareness "can never suffice"[4] to excuse her offense, but writes her essay nevertheless. This tension between a desire to act and an awareness of the problems such action might cause runs through Spivak's essay.

Approach

Spivak's approach is innovative in its combination of different theoretical approaches. Methodologically, "Can the Subaltern Speak?" brings deconstructionist, feminist, and Marxist approaches together in a postcolonial framework. Each of these schools of thought deals with a particular concern; deconstructionism questions assumptions regarding the basic nature of reality by drawing our attention to the role of language in the way that we each construct it, feminism focuses on the marginalization of women, and Marxism focuses on the way in which economics and the struggle between social classes serve to drive history (frequently with a focus on the "proletariat"*—low-paid wage earners). Combining these approaches with a focus on the people of the former colonies, Spivak synthesizes a single, multi-layered approach. The essay's difficulty results, in part, from Spivak fighting several battles at once.

The connections Spivak establishes between gender,* class, and race contributed to the development of what came to be known as "intersectionality."* The term, coined in 1989 by the US lawyer and academic Kimberlé Crenshaw,* refers to the idea that different forms of oppression and marginalization should not, and cannot, be understood in isolation. For example, a working-class black woman finds herself at the intersection of three reasons for marginalization. The interaction and mutual reinforcement of these factors must be taken into account when theorizing a position in society's hierarchy.

Spivak's particular take on intersectionality bears the stamp of deconstructionist thought, by combining deep questioning of categories such as "woman," "black," and "working class." Deconstructionist thinkers are wary of such categories, questioning whether there is such a thing as "black identity" or "working-class experience" that would apply to all black or working-class people. In "Can the Subaltern Speak?" Spivak uses a similar line of questioning to cast doubt on there being a universal experience of subalternity.

Contribution in Context

Spivak's essay is notable for using poststructuralist* philosophy (an approach that questions the possibility of "objective truth"), notably that of Jacques Derrida, for a postcolonial purpose. Spivak had a good knowledge of Derrida's thought, having translated and written a lengthy translator's preface to his book *Of Grammatology* in 1976. While Edward Said had used the theories of Michel Foucault,* another poststructuralist philosopher, in his key postcolonial work *Orientalism*, Spivak was the first to use the work of Derrida. This is important, as the common opinion at the time was that Foucault was concerned with "real history, real politics, and real social problems" whereas Derrida was dismissed as "inaccessible [and] esoteric."[5] In "Can the Subaltern Speak?," however, Spivak argues that Derrida's philosophy is of greater value to debates about the cultural and political legacies of colonialism, and that it retains a "long-term usefulness for people outside the First World" (that is, the developed, rich countries).[6]

In its denial of the possibility of objective truth, Derrida's deconstruction is, in effect, a form of extreme relativism* (the concept that standards of truth and worth are valid only for those who hold them, rather than absolute). For Spivak, deconstruction "is constantly and persistently looking into how truths are produced."[7] This approach seeks to undermine universal claims to value or meaning, and instead shows different competing claims to truth. There is an old joke that says there are three kinds of truth: my truth, your truth, and the truth. Deconstruction takes this one step further, suggesting that there may be my, your, his, her, and any number of other truths, but there is no such thing as "the" truth.

A frequent feature of deconstruction is its questioning of the stability of binary pairs such as men/women, or colonizer/colonized. A common technique of deconstruction is to show that the dominant term in a binary pair—here "men" or "colonizer"—in fact needs its opposite to make sense. Without the colonized, there can be no colonizer; without women, men could not fulfill the roles they do in society, and so the dominant term somehow relies on its opposite. By constantly destabilizing these pairs, deconstruction aims to undermine the stability of hierarchical structures such as colonialism, the class system, and patriarchy.*

NOTES

1   Gayatri Chakravorty Spivak, "Can the Subaltern Speak?," in *Marxism and the Interpretation of Culture* (Basingstoke: Macmillan Education, 1988), 272.

2   Spivak, "Can the Subaltern Speak?," 283.

3   Spivak, "Can the Subaltern Speak?," 271.

4   Spivak, "Can the Subaltern Speak?," 271

5   Spivak, "Can the Subaltern Speak?," 291.

6   Spivak, "Can the Subaltern Speak?," 292.

7   Gayatri Chakravorty Spivak, *The Spivak Reader: Selected Works of Gayati Chakravorty Spivak*, ed. Donna Landry and Gerald MacLean (New York: Routledge, 1995), 28.

SECTION 2
IDEAS

MODULE 5
MAIN IDEAS

KEY POINTS

- The main argument of Gayatri Chakravorty Spivak's essay "Can the Subaltern Speak?" is that subaltern* voices are systematically silenced within existing means of representation—platforms from which one's views and demands are taken seriously.

- The text addresses several main themes: the problems that arise when subalterns are represented by others, the damage caused when the West* assumes its beliefs are held universally, and the doubly oppressed position of subaltern women.

- Spivak has been criticized for how difficult it is to understand her writing. While this may sometimes be justified, her style makes sense in the context of her project of criticism.

Key Themes

Gayatri Chakravorty Spivak defines subalterns as people "removed from all lines of social mobility"[1]—the "illiterate peasantry"[2] who have no access to education or other resources that would allow them to better their position in society. In "Can the Subaltern Speak?" she asks whether it is possible for subalterns to make their voices heard, and so achieve self-representation. Her conclusion is that global structures of power, whether academic, economic, or political, do not at present allow the subaltern to speak.* The word "speak" here means not only to say something, but also to have one's message recognized. Further, any attempt by those with power in society to grant subalterns

" The subaltern cannot speak. "

Gayatri Chakravorty Spivak, "Can the Subaltern Speak?"

collective speech will lead to a distortion of their position, and again deny subalterns the opportunity to speak for themselves.

Spivak's main argument highlights the ethical problems that arise when representing others, or speaking in their place. This may seem surprising, as political representation would appear to be desirable for subalterns, as for any group wishing to better its position in society. But Spivak's point is much broader, suggesting that all forms of representation deny subalterns a fair hearing, and so make their attempts to speak meaningless. It is not that individual subalterns cannot say anything, but rather that speaking from a subaltern's position in society means you will never be heard.

Exploring the Ideas

In the essay, Spivak argues that academic research, colonialism,* and patriarchy* share two common features: a mistaken belief that their values are universal, and a constant silencing of subaltern voices.

Spivak begins by showing how two leading radical intellectuals, the French philosopher Gilles Deleuze* and the historian and theorist Michel Foucault,* underestimate their role in the West's cultural dominance over the rest of the world. These two thinkers, Spivak argues, "systematically ignore the question of ideology and their own implication in intellectual and economic history."[3] That is, they consider themselves to be neutral commentators, when, in fact, they are biased towards the values of the West. This is visible, for example, in their assumption that subalterns from developing nations, typically poor peasants and the urban poor, would have the same political self-consciousness as the Western proletariat* (the working class). This is an unlikely situation, given that poor peasants, the urban poor, and minority members of developing countries typically have considerably less access to education. She further criticizes their use of terms such as "the workers" when writing about the Western proletariat. This, she states, is essentializing*—that is, it reflects a belief that all workers share common, unchanging features.

She then turns to a consideration of different kinds of representation. She cites the German political philosopher Karl Marx's* essay "Eighteenth Brumaire of Louis Bonaparte" (1852), in which Marx writes about how the nephew of Napoleon overthrew the French parliament and declared himself emperor. Spivak points out that while Marx distinguishes between two kinds of representation—*darstellen* (aesthetic representation, such as by painting a picture) and *vertreten* (political representation)—Deleuze and Foucault blur this distinction. As a result, they give the impression that *vertreten*, speaking *for* someone as "a proxy"[4] (that is, as their representative), equates to *darstellen*, a "portrait"[5] of that person and their wishes. The second transforms individuals into symbols of a group, while the first uses that symbol to act on the group's behalf.

For Spivak, blurring these two kinds of representation prevents the critic from exposing the reality—what subalterns actually want— that lies behind representations. Spivak rejects the idea that subalterns can make their own interests known, but also refuses to accept that representation (*vertreten*) can happen ethically. In effect, this part of her argument reinforces her claim that representing (*vertreten*) others leads to a distortion of their position.

In the next section, she gives a detailed critique of the Subaltern Studies Group,* a group of mostly South Asian scholars. She argues that even their seemingly supportive work on subalterns imagines them too much as an undifferentiated mass, that is, it sees all subalterns as the same. To counter this, Spivak says that she uses the term "subaltern" to describe a shifting identity that can have multiple features. As she explains in an interview, her understanding of the word "subaltern" changes according to context.[6] By declaring that "subaltern" has no stable meaning, Spivak adds a greater richness of possibilities to subaltern studies, but arguably gives up the advantages of a clearly defined resistance movement on their behalf.

The final section shows the double difficulty of self-representation for subaltern women. Spivak analyzes the British colonial government in India's banning of *sati** in 1829. *Sati* is a form of widow sacrifice in which a "Hindu widow ascends the pyre [wood pile on which the corpse is burned] of the dead husband and immolates [burns] herself upon it."[7] Although Spivak was probably in favor of ending *sati*, she shows that the process of abolishing it was used to enforce colonial rule, to maintain men's control of women's lives, and to present British civilization in contrast with "savage"[8] Indians. Spivak puts the term "savage" in inverted commas to take ironic distance from it. She uses the language of colonizers, but does so to criticize them, much as she uses the tools of Western philosophy to critique the West.

Spivak also considers the experience of Bhuvaneswari Bhaduri,* a subaltern member of the Indian independence movement, who committed suicide rather than carry out a political assassination in the decades leading up to Indian independence.* As Bhuvaneswari was unable to "speak" through official channels, she resorted to trying to communicate with the only thing she had: her body, by taking her own life. This, for Spivak, presents "a situation where a subaltern person had tried extremely hard to speak, to the extent of making her damned suicide into a message."[9] Her reliance on suicide was "proof" for Spivak that "the subaltern cannot speak,"[10] and especially that the "subaltern as female cannot be heard or read."[11] The voice of the subaltern who is also a woman, for Spivak, is doubly silenced.

Language and Expression

Spivak's essay is written in a complex style that assumes the reader has a working knowledge of concepts from philosophy, Marxism,* the therapeutic theoretical approach known as psychoanalysis,* and feminism.* In a review of a book containing Spivak's essay, the literary critic Terry Eagleton* criticizes a use of language that even "most intellectuals, too, find unintelligible."[12] Spivak herself admits that "I would say that I have a problem, which is that I cannot write clearly."[13]

Spivak's challenging style is not helped by the essay's unusual structure. The argument proceeds by unexpected turns, as often as by logical progression. Frequently, seemingly unrelated topics follow one another, making her argument difficult to follow. While "Can the Subaltern Speak?" requires effort to decode, Spivak's style is perhaps necessary for her project of criticism. Her attempt to question the stability of subaltern identity is matched by her questioning of the stability of language.

What value might a style have that makes complicated ideas seem more complicated? It can be helpful to think of Spivak's writing not as standard academic texts, but rather as something closer to poetry, in which words take on various, often contradictory, roles. Single words—"representation," "subaltern"—have multiple meanings. Much of the work of understanding the essay is left to the reader, a process that is frustrating and rewarding in equal measure.

NOTES

1 Gayatri Chakravorty Spivak, "Scattered Speculations on the Subaltern and the Popular," *Postcolonial Studies: Culture, Politics, Economy* 8, no. 4 (2005): 475.

2 Gayatri Chakravorty Spivak, "Can the Subaltern Speak?," in *Marxism and the Interpretation of Culture* (Basingstoke: Macmillan Education, 1988), 283.

3 Spivak, "Can the Subaltern Speak?," 272.

4 Spivak, "Can the Subaltern Speak?," 276.

5 Spivak, "Can the Subaltern Speak?," 276.

6 Gayatri Chakravorty Spivak, *The Post-colonial Critic: Interviews, Strategies, Dialogues*, ed. Sarah Harasym (London: Routledge, 1990), 141.

7   Spivak, *The Post-colonial Critic*, 141.

8   Spivak, *The Post-colonial Critic*, 301.

9   Gayatri Chakravorty Spivak and Leon de Kock, "Interview with Gayatri Chakravorty Spivak: New Nation Writers Conference in South Africa," *ARIEL: A Review of International English Literature* 23, no. 3 (1992): 44.

10 Spivak and de Kock, "Interview," 44.

11 Spivak, "Can the Subaltern Speak?," 308.

12 Terry Eagleton, "In the Gaudy Supermarket," *London Review of Books* 21, no. 10 (1999): 3.

13 Spivak and de Kock, "Interview," 40.

MODULE 6
SECONDARY IDEAS

KEY POINTS

- The main secondary idea in Spivak's "Can the Subaltern Speak?" is that women subalterns* are doubly disenfranchised or denied a voice.

- For Spivak, patriarchy* and colonialism* work together to oppress women.

- Spivak's concern for early colonial history has not received the attention it deserves. She discusses, for example, how the British colonial masters of India misunderstood the full meaning of ancient Hindu* texts.

Other Ideas

The central concern of Gayatri Chakravorty Spivak's "Can the Subaltern Speak?" is the possibility of subaltern speech in general. But the essay also draws attention to the doubly silenced position of subaltern women. It is important to bear in mind that for Spivak, colonial and patriarchal forms of oppression should not be considered in isolation. They join with one another—and with legal, economic, scholarly, and other systems of power—to produce what, for Spivak, is a global society that is exclusive and repressive to its core. It is not that subaltern women are, on the one hand, victims of colonialism, and, on the other, subject to sexism, but rather that colonial and patriarchal practices work together to silence subaltern women's voices.

As a result, to make certain ideas in Spivak's essay less important is in some measure to be guilty of the hegemonic* tendencies (social structures that serve the dominant classes or cultures) that Spivak criticizes. To decide that this text is mainly about representation—

> **❝** Spivak has further expanded the historical research of the Subaltern Studies historians by focusing on the experiences of subaltern women, which have been effaced in official Indian history. **❞**
>
> Stephen Morton, *Gayatri Chakravorty Spivak*

or the ability of subalterns in general to speak* out—with only a secondary interest in patriarchy, is to impose a reading Spivak would probably resist. With this in mind, Spivak's discussion of women can be considered a part of her broader interest in representation.

Spivak discusses the flaws in methodology of the Subaltern Studies Group*—broadly, their tendency to essentialize* subaltern experience, considering the experience of all subalterns to be essentially the same. In particular, she criticizes them for neglecting the role of women subalterns. She recognizes, however, how difficult it would be to research the role of women subalterns, as the historical records are biased towards men: "If, in the context of colonial production, the subaltern has no history and cannot speak, the subaltern as female is even more deeply in shadow."[1] Records of subaltern women are scarcer than those of male subalterns, making their stories even harder to find.

Exploring the Ideas

To illustrate the double subjugation of subaltern women, Spivak offers the following assessment: "White men are saving brown women from brown men."[2] Spivak here suggests that white men portray Indian men as a threat to Indian women, and so present themselves as acting helpfully by intervening between the two. Underlying this is a belief that white men know what Indian women want, and so can act on their behalf. This is complicated, since the patriarchal nature of Indian society, as Spivak describes it, means that "brown men" do indeed hold power over "brown women." At first glance, for an outside force to intervene in this might appear desirable, but as Spivak notes: "Imperialism's* image as the establisher of the good society is marked by the espousal of the woman as object of protection from her own kind."[3] That is to say, rather than granting women the rights of a subject, who can think and act on her own terms, the colonial governments maintained women as passive objects, and so again denied them independent agency, and the possibility of speaking for themselves.

An important example of this is given when Spivak describes the debate around the banning of *sati** (the burning of widowed women) in 1829. During this debate, colonists and some Hindu men spoke about how women should be treated, but one "never encounters the testimony of the women's voice-consciousness."[4] In other words, women's voices are absent, leaving them doubly excluded as both subalterns and women.

Overlooked

Although Spivak's essay has been widely discussed, some parts of it have not been closely enough examined. In particular, critics have largely neglected her attention to pre-colonial and early-colonial Indian history. In 2000, two scholars observed that the "underread and scarcely commented-on third and fourth sections of Spivak's essay … with their references to the earlier history of British India, have remained resolutely unread in the last ten years."[5] Although it is perhaps an exaggeration to call them "scarcely commented-on," these scholars do offer an alternative way of considering the essay's impact. They suggest that postcolonial criticism has been so concerned with "the temporal frame of European modernity specifically in colonial modernity as a moment of rupture"[6]—that is, colonial history from around the late 1800s to the present—that it has neglected the earlier history of colonialism.

Spivak tries to turn attention to this older history in "Can the Subaltern Speak?" by returning to the ancient texts of the *Rig-Veda* (a collection of roughly 3,000-year-old hymns, used during ceremonies and rites of passage) and the *Dharmasastra* (an ancient book of religious and legal thought that early British colonial administrators mistakenly took to be the book of law for Indian Hindus). Spivak analyses these texts since both were used as evidence during the banning of *sati*. Spivak's typically deconstructionist* approach—she points out how different translations of these text can change their meaning—concludes with the observation that, while the British understood the word *sati* to mean only "widow sacrifice," it also has another, literal meaning: "good wife."[7] This incomplete meaning, mistakenly using *sati* to refer only to "the rite of widow self-immolation," for Spivak "commemorates a grammatical error on the part of the British, quite as the nomenclature [label] 'American Indian' commemorates a factual error on the part of Columbus"[8] (the Italian explorer who thought he had reached India when he had, in fact, reached the Americas). In Spivak's understanding, by substituting "self-immolation on the husband's pyre" for "good-wifehood," the "white men" of the colonial government imposed "a greater ideological constriction" on "brown women."[9] That is, although seemingly acting in these women's interests, the colonial government in fact reinforced their subjugated position.

NOTES

1   Gayatri Chakravorty Spivak, "Can the Subaltern Speak?," in *Marxism and the Interpretation of Culture* (Basingstoke: Macmillan Education, 1988), 287.

2   Spivak, "Can the Subaltern Speak?," 296.

3   Spivak, "Can the Subaltern Speak?," 299.

4   Spivak, "Can the Subaltern Speak?," 297.

5   Sandhya Shetty and Elizabeth Jane Bellamy, "Postcolonialism's Archive Fever," *Diacritics* 30, no. 1 (2000): 25–8.

6   Shetty and Bellamy, "Postcolonialism's Archive Fever," 28.

7   Spivak, "Can the Subaltern Speak?," 305.

8   Spivak, "Can the Subaltern Speak?," 305.

9   Spivak, "Can the Subaltern Speak?," 305.

ACHIEVEMENT

KEY POINTS

- "Can the Subaltern Speak?" succeeded in revealing the silencing of subaltern* voices. However, the success of its implicit goal—to make them heard—is less certain.

- The rise of both literary theory* (the reading of literary texts using certain philosophical approaches to understanding culture and language) and a new wave of feminism* acknowledging the situation of non-Western women helped Spivak's essay to be recognized and valued in the 1980s.

- Spivak's deconstructionist* approach, with its difficult-to-grasp, shifting analysis, has arguably limited the concrete political value of her text.

Assessing the Argument

If Gayatri Chakravorty Spivak's aim in "Can the Subaltern Speak?" is understood as being to show that subaltern voices are systematically silenced, she is largely successful. She presents a body of evidence ranging from radical philosophy to Marxist* theory, from feminist criticism and revisionist* (reexamined) history to colonial legislation, all of which indicate that the voice of the subaltern has been silenced. She shows that worldwide historical, economic, legal, and ideological* factors have combined, to "obstruct the possibility of being heard"—that is, the possibility of speaking* to a willing listener—for those who "inhabit the periphery."[1] By this she means those who live outside the West,* particularly the poor and excluded within those non–Western societies.

> ❝ Who the hell wants to museumize or protect subalternity? Only extremely reactionary, dubious anthropologistic museumizers. No activist wants to keep the subaltern in the space of difference. To do a thing, to work for the subaltern, means to bring it into speech. ❞
>
> Gayatri Chakravorty Spivak and Leon de Kock, "Interview with Gayatri Chakravorty Spivak"

"Can the Subaltern Speak?" succeeds in offering an abstract understanding of the way the language of those with authority and power keeps subalterns down. Spivak's text certainly helps to undermine the logic behind essentializing* representations—that is, representations that reduce individuals to crude stereotypes. Yet the essay has had a limited effect in ending such behaviors. At best, the essay may have encouraged sensitivity to the compromised position that intellectuals occupy when they speak in the place of silenced subalterns. Academics are now, hopefully, more aware that speaking in the place of subalterns brings with it the possibility of misrepresentation—of not being accurate when trying to explain the thoughts and interests of the poor and excluded. Nevertheless, the fact that Spivak has frequently returned to this text—she has published revised versions—suggests her belief in its ongoing importance to current issues. If her intention is to raise a question that continues to be relevant even in light of changing cultural and historical developments, she has been successful.

Achievement in Context

"Can the Subaltern Speak?" is very much a product of its time. It appeared as the influence of literary theory (very broadly, a range of critical approaches to reading texts that pay attention to larger concepts such as language, gender,* race, interpretation, or society) was on the rise in American and European (particularly British) universities. From the early 1980s, radical journals such as *Critical Inquiry* and *October* published texts by thinkers such as Jacques Derrida,* Jacques Lacan,* Michel Foucault,* Walter Benjamin* and others, which sparked an interest in what the writings of these philosophers and theorists might mean for the study of literature and culture.

In her essay, Spivak takes a number of approaches that were circulating in literary theory at the time—deconstruction, feminism, Marxism— and uses them for a postcolonial* critique. The fact that academics were open to approaches informed by literary theory during the 1980s and 1990s offered the ideal context for the reception of a theoretically dense work like "Can the Subaltern Speak?" The success of Spivak's essay rests partly on the academic world being primed with the ideas of literary theory before her essay's appearance.

The field of postcolonial studies in the late 1980s and early 1990s was flourishing, meaning that Spivak's essay was widely distributed, republished, and discussed in influential critical works and collections of important postcolonial texts such as *The Empire Writes Back* (1989) and *The Post-colonial Studies Reader* (1995).[2] Further, the early 1990s saw the rise of third-wave feminism, which broadened the scope of feminism to incorporate the concerns of women of different cultural backgrounds, sexualities, and races. Spivak's essay also found considerable traction in this area of study, meaning her work was picked up in different fields shortly after its publication. Third-wave feminists took particular inspiration from Spivak's sensitivity to the nuances of race and class when conducting feminist analysis.

Limitations

Although the majority of Spivak's examples in "Can the Subaltern Speak?" are drawn from Indian culture, the problems of representation it identifies, and its anti-essentialist methodology (insisting subalterns can have different desires and interests), are designed to be adaptable to different parts of the world, and different historical periods. It is crucial to bear in mind, however, that this essay is not a guide for action that can be used in any situation. Spivak specifies in the essay that "the Indian case cannot be taken as representative of all countries, nations, cultures, and the like that may be invoked as the Other* of Europe as Self."[3] Spivak warns that just because both Indian subalterns and those in other countries may be similarly marginalized, this does not mean their situation is the same. Spivak describes her position as a "a classic deconstructive" one, which in this case means one that seeks to solve problems "situationally, and not for ever."[4] No solution is ever the ideal solution for all times and places, and solutions will have to be adapted to meet changing historical, political, and geographical conditions.

Spivak's lack of commitment to a single, stable methodology is at once the essay's strength and its weakness. By offering a shifting framework of interpretation, she gets round the problem that fixed frameworks do not fit all examples. However, by never defining exactly what it is we should do in situations concerning subalternity, this approach can feel worryingly without direction or form. Further, if every method and every stable point of meaning are to be undermined, this raises the question of why a deconstructive methodology should be used. If we are to doubt everything, should we not doubt deconstruction's questioning of stability as much as we question stable meaning itself?

NOTES

1   Rosalind C. Morris, ed., *Can the Subaltern Speak? Reflections on the History of an Idea* (New York: Columbia University Press, 2010), back matter.

2   Bill Ashcroft, Gareth Griffiths, and Helen Tiffin, *The Empire Writes Back* (London: Routledge, 1989); Bill Ashcroft, Gareth Griffiths, and Helen Tiffin, eds., *The Post-colonial Studies Reader* (London: Taylor & Francis, 1995).

3   Gayatri Chakravorty Spivak, "Can the Subaltern Speak?," in *Marxism and the Interpretation of Culture* (Basingstoke: Macmillan Education, 1988), 281.

4   Gayatri Chakravorty Spivak and Leon de Kock, "Interview with Gayatri Chakravorty Spivak: New Nation Writers Conference in South Africa," *ARIEL: A Review of International English Literature* 23, no. 3 (1992): 39.

PLACE IN THE AUTHOR'S WORK

KEY POINTS

- The core project of "Can the Subaltern Speak?"—to highlight the silencing of subalterns* and so move towards subaltern self-representation—has remained consistent across Spivak's work.

- Gayatri Chakravorty Spivak has not concentrated on practical solutions. But one suggestion she has often made is for Western scholars to learn a language of the South, thereby opening the possibility of dialogue with some subalterns.

- If Spivak's contribution to scholarship is considered outside the field of postcolonial* studies, her most important publication is probably her translation of Jacques Derrida's* *Of Grammatology.*

Positioning

Gayatri Chakravorty Spivak's "Can the Subaltern Speak?" was first published in the journal *Wedge* in 1985. She published an extended version in *Marxism and the Interpretation of Culture* in 1988, and then rewrote it for her book *A Critique of Postcolonial Reason: Towards a History of the Vanishing Present* (1999). As recently as 2010 she wrote a response to a collection of works reflecting on the history of her essay.[1] In short, although a relatively early work, this essay has been a frequent feature of Spivak's academic career.

However, it does not exist in a vacuum. Prior to this essay she published several articles, notably "French Feminism in an International Frame," and "Three Women's Texts and a Critique of

> 66 'Can the Subaltern Speak?' is perhaps the most famous and controversial work that Spivak has produced. 99
>
> Stephen Morton, *Gayatri Chakravorty Spivak*

Imperialism,"[2] which focus on postcolonial and feminist* approaches to literary texts. The next major landmark in Spivak's career that had a direct impact on "Can the Subaltern Speak?" was her translation from the original French to English of Jacques Derrida's *Of Grammatology* in 1976. It included her extensive translator's introduction in which she provided an analysis of the work. The anti-essentialist* methods of deconstruction* that she discovered when translating Derrida's work came to influence "Can the Subaltern Speak?"

Integration

On the surface Spivak's theoretical approach can seem confused—she calls herself a "theoretical gadfly" and a "bricoleur"[3] (someone who creates from whatever random materials are to hand). Yet there is a steady concern in her work that holds it together in a deeper way. This is summarized in just a few words by the critic Stephen Morton, who identifies the driving force behind Spivak's works as being "to learn to learn from the subaltern."[4] One notable way she has sought to achieve this in recent years is her call to "learn well one of the languages of the rural poor of the South."[5] Although this will never offer a solution to all social ills, it is at least a logical first step, as it opens the possibility of dialogue with subalterns. This is not, however, the endpoint of Spivak's project. In addition to finding ways to allow subaltern speech, it is also necessary to work "against subalternity."[6] This means establishing global systems of economic organization and political representation in which the category of the subaltern ceases to exist.

Spivak's commitment to promoting the rights of the excluded began before "Can the Subaltern Speak?" and has continued in her later work. In one part of her essay "Three Women's Texts and a Critique of Imperialism,"[7] Spivak reads the Victorian novelist Charlotte Brontë's* *Jane Eyre.** Her purpose is to show that the novel's seemingly positive feminist politics, which depict white women as active agents, also serve to marginalize a Creole* (mixed race) woman. *Jane Eyre* describes the story of a Western woman coming to adulthood, but Spivak argues that this development is only possible due to the oppression of another character, a non-Western woman. Such readings—against the grain of the literary canon* (the books considered the best examples of Western literature)—are typical of Spivak's approach.

In a similar manner to her approach in "Can the Subaltern Speak?," Spivak here insists on a multi-layered approach that is at once feminist and postcolonial. In her later work, such as her 1999 book *A Critique of Postcolonial Reason*, Spivak shows the ethnocentric* biases in the history of the European branch of philosophy known as metaphysics* ("ethnocentric" here refers to assumptions regarding the superiority of a specific ethnic group). She also argues that the field of postcolonial studies has itself become involved in harmful practices of knowledge production about the Global South* by producing research about poor countries in a way that hurts their interests.

Some of her most recent work, such as the 2003 collection *Death of a Discipline*, proposes that comparative literature must move beyond a narrow focus on literatures in European languages to include "the languages of the Southern Hemisphere."[8] While this may seem of restricted political scope, it shows that, in Morton's words, an "ethical commitment to the subaltern in Spivak's thought is increasingly linked to questions of translation and transnational literacy."[9] This suggests an effort to learn the languages of subalterns, and so find a way of engaging with subaltern cultures that is more ethically sound. The question of language, already visible in her discussion of the translation and origins of the word *sati** in "Can the Subaltern Speak?," has remained a constant feature of her intellectual project.

While Spivak has used various approaches, the core project of "Can the Subaltern Speak?"—to draw attention to the marginalization of people who can be considered subaltern, and so promote their agency—has remained consistent across her work.

Significance

If Spivak is seen as a postcolonial theorist, it is safe to say that "Can the Subaltern Speak?" is her best-known and most important work. Spivak, however, resists being pigeonholed as a postcolonial theorist. In one relatively early interview in 1993 she described herself as a "para-disciplinary, ethical philosopher,"[10] although she would later reject this title. "Can the Subaltern Speak?" is a central pillar of postcolonial studies, and when it was published it was immediately recognized as an important contribution to the field. As its frequent reprinting and inclusion in anthologies shows, this importance has lasted. One key factor that contributed to the longevity of the essay is Spivak's choice to frame it as a question. Her answer to it in the late 1980s—that the subaltern cannot speak*—was only ever meant to be true in a certain context, at a certain time. It is a question that is good to repeat regularly, and Spivak's essay provides some guidance for what we should consider when trying to answer it for ourselves.

If Spivak's influence on scholarship is considered more broadly, it is arguably the case that her translation of Derrida's *Of Grammatology* has been her most influential work. It profoundly shaped the branch of postcolonial studies informed by poststructuralist* philosophy—which rejects the idea of universal truth, a crucial part of postcolonial rejections of Eurocentric* thought (thought that assumes the primacy of European perspectives). Her translation also introduced this important French philosopher to an English-speaking audience for the first time. Thanks in large part to Spivak's translation and critical introduction, Derrida's work is now widely cited in diverse fields, including the fields of English literature, history, and philosophy.

NOTES

1   Gayatri Chakravorty Spivak, "In Response: Looking Back, Looking Forward," in *Can the Subaltern Speak? Reflections on the History of an Idea*, ed. Rosalind C. Morris (New York: Columbia University Press, 2010), 227–36.

2   Gayatri Chakravorty Spivak, "French Feminism in an International Frame," *Yale French Studies*, no. 62 (1981); Gayatri Chakravorty Spivak, "Three Women's Texts and a Critique of Imperialism," *Critical Inquiry* 12, no. 1 (1985).

3   Spivak, *The Post-colonial Critic*, 55.

4   Gayatri Chakravorty Spivak, *The Post-colonial Critic: Interviews, Strategies, Dialogues*, ed. Sarah Harasym (London: Routledge, 1990),160.

5   Gayatri Chakravorty Spivak, "Righting Wrongs," in *Human Rights, Human Wrongs: Oxford Amnesty Lectures 2001*, ed. Nicholas Owen (Oxford: Oxford University Press, 2003), 208.

6   Gayatri Chakravorty Spivak and Leon de Kock, "Interview with Gayatri Chakravorty Spivak: New Nation Writers Conference in South Africa," *ARIEL: A Review of International English Literature* 23, no. 3 (1992): 46.

7   Spivak, "Three Women's Texts and a Critique of Imperialism," 262.

8   Gayatri Chakravorty Spivak, *Death of a Discipline* (New York: Columbia University Press, 2003), 9.

9   Stephen Morton, *Gayatri Spivak: Ethics, Subalternity and the Critique of Postcolonial Reason* (Cambridge: Polity, 2007), 162.

10 Gayatri Chakravorty Spivak, Sara Danius, and Stefan Jonsson, "An Interview with Gayatri Chakravorty Spivak," *Boundary 2* 20, no. 2 (1993): 25.

SECTION 3
IMPACT

MODULE 9
THE FIRST RESPONSES

KEY POINTS

- "Can the Subaltern Speak?" has been criticized both for the difficulty of its language, and for Spivak's deconstructionist* approach, which suggests to some readers that it is not even worth trying to give the subaltern* a voice, since such efforts are doomed to failure.

- The most important responses to Spivak's critics come from Spivak herself. She has clarified and defended her essay in interviews and modified versions, and later taken on board the earlier criticisms.

- The conflict between poststructuralist* and Marxist* strands of postcolonial* studies has been crucial in shaping the debate about "Can the Subaltern Speak?" At the same time, this essay has shaped the debate in postcolonial studies.

Criticism

Gayatri Chakravorty Spivak's "Can the Subaltern Speak?" was met with mixed responses. The historian Gyan Prakash, writing in 1992, saw the value that Spivak's deconstructionist approach might have for the study of history. For Prakash: "Spivak very correctly marks the silencing of the subaltern woman as the point at which the interpreter must acknowledge the limits of historical understanding; it is impossible to retrieve the woman's voice when she was not given a subject-position from which to speak."*[1] Prakash here accepts the validity of Spivak's challenge to historians who attempt to "retrieve the … voice" of subaltern women. This implies that education, legal

> ❝[C]ritics of Spivak's work are skeptical of whether Spivak's deconstructive reading strategies achieve anything other than a theoretical paralysis of effective political intervention.❞
>
> Stephen Morton, *Gayatri Chakravorty Spivak*

equality, economic opportunities, and political reform must be in place before one can imagine such women finding their voices.

The historian Partha Chatterjee,* a member of the Subaltern Studies Group,* observes: "Initially in our thinking, subalternity still referred to a certain class structure that was perhaps not entirely frozen or well-defined." But "Gayatri Spivak's interventions" allowed a consideration of "subalternity as something that adheres to an individual," and so "added a completely new dimension to … subalternity."[2] In short, Spivak's insistence on the heterogeneity of subaltern groups (that is, the wide differences between and inside of subaltern groups) was incorporated into the methodology of some members of the group. After Spivak, to be a subaltern was no longer just to occupy a class position; it was also to have an individual identity.

The Indian gender* and postcolonialist studies scholar Ania Loomba offers a more combative response to Spivak's essay. She appreciates Spivak's demonstration that the "absence of women's voices in the colonial debate" shows the "difficulty of recovering subject positions in general" (that is, the difficulty of discovering the experiences and concerns of people who have been without a voice), noting that this indicates the "violence of colonialism* and of indigenous patriarchy* in particular."[3] But she finds Spivak's conclusion that the subaltern *cannot* speak "disquieting for those who are engaged in precisely the task of recovering such voices."[4] For Loomba, Spivak's insistence on the subaltern's lack of a voice is proved wrong by the fact that scholarship in this area is indeed taking place.

A number of commentators, particularly some Marxists and feminists,* were hostile to Spivak's deconstructionist approach, which for them suggests that subalterns do not and cannot play a political role. In her 1987 essay "Problems in Current Theories of Political Discourse," the literary theorist Benita Parry argues that in deciding that the subaltern cannot speak, Spivak offers a "deliberated deafness to the native voice where it is to be heard."[5] Parry thinks Spivak's approach leads to the discourses* of colonialism—the way colonialists maintain power through language—preventing all possible forms of resistance. These critics fault Spivak for ignoring the voices of the poor and excluded where they can, in fact, be heard.

Responses

Spivak has responded to criticisms—and to what she considers misunderstandings—of her essay, addressing both theoretical objections and criticism of her style. When asked how she responded to criticism of her conclusion that the subaltern was silenced, she offered her own criticism of those who confuse subalterns speaking with subalterns being heard. Further, she showed that people sometimes mistakenly think that subalterns are speaking out, when in reality, those speaking out are wrongly claiming subaltern status. Those, for example, who are "just … a discriminated against minority on the university campus"[6] may be oppressed, but they are not experiencing subalternity: a position of much greater powerlessness.

Around 10 years after the essay was published, Spivak made substantial changes to her position, recognizing that it was indeed written in a way that was needlessly hard to understand. In one interview, she refers to "a turgid piece called 'Can the Subaltern Speak?',"[7] and in a different interview, she states that the original was "too complicated"[8] and had led to misunderstandings. This suggests Spivak distancing herself from the style of the earlier version, as she criticizes its pomposity and difficulty.

In 1999, she published a revised and extended version of the essay, in which she clarifies her style and notes that saying "the subaltern cannot speak" was "an inadvisable remark."[9] In the revised version, Spivak doubts her original conclusion, stating that "when a line of communication is established between a member of subaltern groups and the circuits of citizenship and institutionality, the subaltern has been inserted into the long road to hegemony."*[10] In other words, when subalterns communicate with those who are not subalterns, this begins a process of overcoming subalternity. This change is enormously important, as it suggests a possible way out of subalternity. Establishing such lines of communication, Spivak continues, is "absolutely to be desired,"[11] unless we are "romantic purists or primitivists about 'preserving subalternity'."[12] Once again, Spivak's goal is firstly to make subalterns heard—but its longer-term aim is to rid the world of subalternity altogether and no longer to have groups of poor and excluded people living with no way to express their demands and have them heard.

Conflict and Consensus

The debate around the project of social criticism and the language of "Can the Subaltern Speak?" remains unresolved. This is visible in a number of spheres. The positions broadly represented by Spivak's approach, labeled deconstructive discourse analysis,* and early Marxist critics of Spivak, such as Parry, have come to mark a split in postcolonial studies.

Very broadly speaking, postcolonial studies is now divided into two camps. On the one hand are approaches informed by poststructural philosophy and discourse analysis, which are most interested in linguistic "epistemic violence"* (violence carried out through language, but that can lead to physical violence). On the other are Marxist approaches that examine the political and historical reality of resistance and conflict. Spivak's work is strongly associated with the poststructuralist strand of postcolonial studies, which some Marxist postcolonial scholars consider too abstract to have any practical application. The debate over the political effectiveness of Spivak's essay in part defined the current shape of postcolonial studies.

Debates over the accessibility of Spivak's work also continue. This question of accessibility (how difficult or easy it is to understand the text), although perhaps less theoretically interesting, is a particularly sore point in postcolonial studies. If one of the goals of postcolonial studies is to provide oppressed, often semi-literate or illiterate, people with the critical tools to rid themselves of oppression, the accessibility of these texts is of key importance. In a hostile review of *A Critique of Postcolonial Reason* (which contains the revised version of the essay), the literary critic Terry Eagleton* scolds Spivak for her "obscurantism"[13]—for making the text needlessly complicated. The feminist critic Judith Butler* writes in response, however, that "the wide-ranging audience for Spivak's work proves that spoon-feeding is less appreciated than forms of activist thinking and writing that challenge us to think the world more radically."[14] Butler argues that, while there are simpler ways of writing, Spivak's dense style offers an interesting stimulus for thought.

NOTES

1   Gyan Prakash, "Postcolonial Criticism and Indian Historiography," *Social Text*, no. 31/32 (1992): 12.

2   Gyanendra Pandey, Partha Chatterjee, and Moyukh Chatterjee, "Reflecting on 30 Years of Subaltern Studies: Conversations with Profs. Gyanendra Pandey and Partha Chatterjee," accessed October 14, 2015, http://www.culanth.org/curated_collections/6-subaltern-studies/discussions/14-reflecting-on-30-years-of-subaltern-studies-conversations-with-profs-gyanendra-pandey-and-partha-chatterjee.

3   Ania Loomba, "Dead Women Tell No Tales: Issues of Female Subjectivity, Subaltern Agency and Tradition in Colonial and Post-colonial Writings on Widow Immolation in India," *History Workshop*, no. 36 (1993): 217.

4   Loomba, "Dead Women Tell No Tales," 218.

5   Benita Parry, "Problems in Current Theories of Colonial Discourse," *Oxford Literary Review* 9, no. 1 (1987): 39.

6   Gayatri Chakravorty Spivak and Leon de Kock, "Interview with Gayatri Chakravorty Spivak: New Nation Writers Conference in South Africa," *ARIEL: A Review of International English Literature* 23, no. 3 (1992): 46.

7   Gayatri Chakravorty Spivak, "Diasporas Old and New: Women in the Transnational World," *Textual Practice* 10, no. 2 (1996): 262.

8   Gayatri Chakravorty Spivak, *The Spivak Reader: Selected Works of Gayati Chakravorty Spivak*, ed. Donna Landry and Gerald MacLean (New York: Routledge, 1995), 288.

9   Gayatri Chakravorty Spivak, *A Critique of Postcolonial Reason: Toward a History of the Vanishing Present* (Cambridge, MA: Harvard University Press, 1999), 308.

10 Spivak, *A Critique of Postcolonial Reason*, 310.

11 Spivak, *A Critique of Postcolonial Reason*, 310.

12 Spivak, *A Critique of Postcolonial Reason*, 310.

13 Terry Eagleton, "In the Gaudy Supermarket," *London Review of Books* 21, no. 10 (1999).

14 Judith Butler, "Exacting Solidarities," *London Review of Books* 21, no. 13 (1999): 2.

THE EVOLVING DEBATE

KEY POINTS

- Gayatri Chakravorty Spivak shows flexibility in her thinking by promoting "strategic essentialism."* It suggests temporarily putting aside the critique of essentialism (the assumption that a subject can be defined by its essential characteristics) in order to unite with others with a similar identity to achieve a political goal.

- Spivak has had a big impact on feminist* theory, inspiring academics to be more sensitive to the needs of women who are not Western and middle class.

- The legacy of Spivak's work is felt strongly, both in the academic world, and among the subalterns* with whom she has worked.

Uses and Problems

Gayatri Chakravorty Spivak's "Can the Subaltern Speak?" raised concerns among scholars about the ethical dilemmas that arise when they speak* in place of their subaltern subjects of research. Spivak's decision to focus on the most powerless groups in society brought about a change in how the study of marginalized people was understood. At the same time, the essay marked an early step in the ongoing process of bringing postcolonial* concerns into the practice of scholarship more widely.

The essay's critique of essentialism—the belief that certain peoples share an unchanging "nature"—takes on a different character in her concept of "strategic essentialism."[1]

The term describes a process of suspending the knowledge

> **❝** The idea of strategic essentialism accepts that essentialist categories of human identity should be criticized, but emphasizes that one cannot avoid using such categories at times in order to make sense of the social and political world. **❞**
>
> Stephen Morton, *Gayatri Chakravorty Spivak*

that essentialism is a myth in order to achieve some political goal. Some feminist theorists, for example, might question the notion that womanhood is a natural state rather than a learned set of behaviors. The French thinker Simone de Beauvoir* famously said, "One is not born, but rather becomes, a woman,"[2] meaning that one learns how to be a woman by living in society rather than naturally by being born female. But in certain circumstances, it might be politically helpful for women to act as if they shared a common identity—in order to mobilize all women in a feminist political campaign, for example. While Spivak argues that there is a wide range of identities among subalterns, she recognizes in her essay "Deconstructing Historiography"[3] that there are instances when it would be helpful for subalterns to act as a group in order to have greater political leverage.

Drawing on deconstructionist* techniques, Spivak is highly suspicious of any talk of innate essence—the idea that various groups of people have a natural, unchanging identity; indeed, a large part of her work is devoted to undoing such essentialist beliefs. But Spivak is also politically motivated, and is sometimes willing to suspend her anti-essentialism temporarily if it can achieve a valuable political outcome such as helping subalterns achieve greater self-representation.

Schools of Thought
One notable area in which Spivak's thought has gained traction is in feminist studies. In her essay, Spivak touches on the dangers

of a feminism blind to the differences between the needs of First World women (that is, those from the rich countries) and women from developing nations. "Clearly," Spivak notes, "if you are poor, black, and female you get it in three ways."[4] Although only touched on briefly in "Can the Subaltern Speak?," this idea would become increasingly important in her later scholarship.

Spivak's concern for anti-essentialism and strategic essentialism has been taken up by feminist scholars in works such as the collection of essays *Feminist Genealogies, Colonial Legacies, Democratic Futures* (1997). As in Spivak's essay, Jacqui Alexander and Chandra Talpade Mohanty argue here that the experiences of white middle-class women should not dictate the project of feminism. Instead, they call for a "transnational feminism" that proposes "a way of thinking about women in similar contexts across the world, in *different* geographical spaces, rather than as all women across the world."[5] If, as de Beauvoir implies, we are not born but learn to be women, we must recognize that this happens differently in different regions, and feminist criticism should be sensitive to this. It might do this by recognizing that, for example, a Bengali woman's sense of herself as a woman might differ from that of a woman in the West,* and so the solutions it proposes for their emancipation should be tailored to each context.

The leading feminist critic Judith Butler* draws directly on Spivak's ideas in her pioneering book *Bodies that Matter: On the Discursive Limits of "Sex"* (1993).[6] It begins with part of an interview with Spivak, quoting her speaking about the deconstructionist approach. Butler uses Spivak's methods as the foundation of her own efforts to reevaluate sexual difference by looking at the role of power in the construction of gender.* Butler suggests that we "provisionally … institute an identity and at the same time … open the category as a site of permanent political contest."[7] Butler here is calling for the use of Spivak's strategic essentialism, both as a way to achieve a political goal, and as a way of making gender identities a political topic for debate. In this way, Butler hopes to bring concerns of gender into the public sphere.*

In Current Scholarship

"Can the Subaltern Speak?" has been highly influential on the work of scholars. Butler praises Spivak's influence as "unparalleled by any living scholar." She adds that Spivak has "changed the academic terrain"[8] of feminist theory, Marxist* theory and subaltern studies. The essay can be felt in the work of historians, cultural theorists, geographers, and anthropologists, and it continues to be taught and read on university courses. In a very recent adaptation of Spivak's thought, the scholar Yahu T. Vinayaraj published the article "Spivak, Feminism, and Theology,"[9] examining the significance that the deconstructive approach of Spivak's essay might have for current feminist theology (the systematic study of religious ideas, commonly drawing on religious literature such as the Bible).

The conclusions Spivak comes to in this essay have also had more immediate practical consequences. Another important group that continues Spivak's project are the subaltern women with whom she works. While Spivak's theorizing is aimed at an educated academic audience, this is complemented by her hands-on activism. She spends time each year in West Bengal and Bangladesh where she runs a literacy project and seeks to promote "the habit of democracy."[10] By working directly with these women over a long period, Spivak learns with subalterns, helping them shape their desires and learn how to translate them into political change.

NOTES

1   Gayatri Chakravorty Spivak, "Deconstructing Historiography," in *Selected Subaltern Studies*, ed. Ranajit Guha and Gayatri Chakravorty Spivak (New Delhi: Oxford University Press, n.d.), 3.

2   Simone de Beauvoir, *The Second Sex* (New York: Vintage, 1973), 301.

3   Spivak, "Deconstructing Historiography."

4   Gayatri Chakravorty Spivak, "Can the Subaltern Speak?," in *Marxism and the Interpretation of Culture* (Basingstoke: Macmillan Education, 1988), 294.

5   M. Jacqui Alexander and Chandra Talpade Mohanty, eds., "Introduction: Genealogies, Legacies, Movements," in *Feminist Genealogies, Colonial Legacies, Democratic Futures* (New York; London: Routledge, 1997), xix.

6   Judith Butler, *Bodies that Matter: On the Discursive Limits of "Sex"* (New York; London: Routledge, 1993).

7   Butler, *Bodies that Matter*, 222.

8   Judith Butler, "Exacting Solidarities," *London Review of Books* 21, no. 13 (1999).

9   Yahu T. Vinayaraj, "Spivak, Feminism, and Theology," *Feminist Theology* 22, no. 2 (2014).

10 Gayatri Chakravorty Spivak and Nazish Brohi, "In Conversation with Gayatri Spivak," *Dawn*, accessed October 15, 2015, http://www.dawn.com/news/1152482.

MODULE 11
IMPACT AND INFLUENCE TODAY

KEY POINTS

- "Can the Subaltern Speak?" is still stimulating study and debate. Although it was written about India, it has been widely cited in the study of subalterns* in other parts of the world.

- The essay's examination of how subalterns attempt to communicate when their voices are silenced remains relevant to current concerns.

- Some critics question whether Spivak's deconstructive* approach has brought about much positive change for subalterns since the essay's publication.

Position

On the 20th anniversary of the publication of Gayatri Chakravorty Spivak's "Can the Subaltern Speak?," the anthropologist Rosalind Morris organized a conference on the text. This led to the publication of the volume of essays *Can the Subaltern Speak? Reflections on the History of an Idea* (2010), which intended to evaluate the continuing impact of Spivak's essay. As Morris writes, the conference "marked no (anticipated) diminution in the pace or output of Spivak's continued writing," and was instead an "effort to grasp, once again, the full implications of her insistent and uncompromising introduction of the questions of gender* and sexual difference into the critique of radical discourse."[1] In the collection, the importance of Spivak's essay is not limited to the immediate Indian context that "Can the Subaltern Speak?" describes. The collection contains an essay on subaltern studies after Spivak by Partha Chatterjee,*[2] a member of the Subaltern Studies Group.* Another by Peng Cheah,

> **❝** [T]hough 'Can the Subaltern Speak?' answered its own question in the negative, its corollary question, How can we learn to listen? remains radically open. **❞**
>
> Rosalind C. Morris, *Can the Subaltern Speak? Reflections on the History of an Idea*

"Biopower and the New International Division of Reproductive Labour,"[3] considers the Marxist* aspects of Spivak's text in the context of Singapore, the Philippines, and other Southeast Asian countries.

In one interesting contribution, "Moving from Subalternity: Indigenous Women in Guatemala and Mexico," the British-born literary critic Jean Franco considers how Spivak's ideas might be adapted for regions of Latin America.[4] She also makes the case for reading particular kinds of subaltern silence as secrecy rather than voicelessness (the inability to speak*). As she notes, "secrecy is a strategy of defense of community customs that seeks to make them invulnerable to outside scrutiny."[5] By hiding the truth through silence or disguise, subalterns might protect themselves from forms of epistemic violence.* By taking this approach, Franco shows how the silence of subalterns can, in certain circumstances, be read as deliberate use agency (the ability to act on a decision) rather than simply as an effect of marginalization (being excluded and therefore unable to speak out). By withholding knowledge about themselves, subalterns can regain some degree of control over how they are represented in the West.*

Interaction
While some have treated Spivak's question of subaltern speech as a purely theoretical one, others have engaged with the political consequences of the question, and have used Spivak's essay as inspiration, even if it cannot be seen as direct guidance.

In their article "Can the Subaltern Vote?" the scholars Leerom Medovoi, Shankar Raman, and Benjamin Johnson argue that while the 1990 elections in Nicaragua might appear as an instance of subalterns expressing agency, the meaning of the vote was misunderstood by the American press, and so the message was effectively silenced. Nicaraguans were tired after years of a US economic embargo and war waged by the Contras—US-sponsored right-wing rebels. The article argues that by voting in a center-right alliance in 1990, Nicaraguans were as much seeking to end US aggression as opposing the ruling left-wing Sandinista party. In the words of the article, they voted to communicate a "complex statement regarding the political, economic, and military subordination of Nicaragua to US capital and geopolitics." But the American press heard only "the simple voice of Nicaraguan sovereignty."[6] It is important to remember that for Spivak, to "speak" in its full sense requires to be heard, and so to "vote" would require having the meaning of that vote understood. For Medovoi and his colleagues, the institutional misunderstanding of this vote offers an instance of subaltern silencing.

Some of the concerns of "Can the Subaltern Speak?" reemerged in 2002, when Spivak gave a paper on "Terror" in the wake of the attacks on targets in New York and Washington, notably the World Trade Center, on September 11, 2001.* While Spivak states clearly that she does not "endorse suicide bombing," and that she is a pacifist, she felt it important to "imagine what message [their suicide attack] might contain."[7] Here Spivak's thinking returns to the description of the suicide of Bhuvaneswari Bhaduri* given in the final section of "Can the Subaltern Speak?," in which she tried to understand how, in desperation, a person might use their own life to try to communicate (Bhaduri hanged herself in 1926 as a way of expressing her unwillingness to carry out a political assassination).

The Continuing Debate

Spivak's essay in part founded the now dominant branch of postcolonial* studies, informed by poststructuralist* thought, in which critics read texts for instances of "instability, ambivalence … the in-between."[8] This approach uses Spivak's deconstructive method to analyze texts, and question the stability of meaning. Some critics have found this kind of criticism too abstract, however, and too far removed from the daily realities of the postcolonial world.

The postcolonial theorist Neil Lazarus has gone as far as to suggest that by reading all postcolonial texts through this same deconstructive lens, such criticism in fact performs the kind of universalizing* it tries to criticize. In his recent *The Postcolonial Unconscious* (2011),[9] Lazarus argues that postcolonial literature offers an extraordinary variety of styles and genres. By coming to similar conclusions about all these texts—such as a conclusion showing that the subaltern is always rendered silent—deconstructionist critics impose readings on these texts that do not reflect what they are actually saying. In short, the voice of the postcolonial text is silenced by academic critics—often Western and privileged.

Other critics, such as the Marxist literary theorist Aijaz Ahmad,* have questioned the value of postcolonial theory based on poststructuralism, given that it has accomplished little in terms of improving the lot of postcolonial peoples.[10] Ahmad suggests that after some 30 years of trying a poststructuralist approach with little success, it might be time to adopt different strategies. In Ahmad's understanding, questions of discourse should be secondary to those of economics. In his words: "Postcoloniality is … like most things, a matter of class."[11] By this, he means that without addressing the imbalance of power caused by the uneven distribution of wealth in society, any attempt to break down the systems in which certain nations or cultures dominate will fail.

NOTES

1   Rosalind C. Morris, ed., *Can the Subaltern Speak? Reflections on the History of an Idea* (New York: Columbia University Press, 2010), 1.

2   Partha Chatterjee, "Reflections on 'Can the Subaltern Speak?': Subaltern Studies after Spivak," in *Can the Subaltern Speak? Reflections on the History of an Idea*, ed. Rosalind C. Morris (New York: Columbia University Press, 2010), 81–6.

3   Peng Cheah, "Biopower and the New International Division of Reproductive Labour," in *Can the Subaltern Speak? Reflections on the History of an Idea*, ed. Rosalind C. Morris (New York: Columbia University Press, 2010), 179–212.

4   Jean Franco, "Moving from Subalternity: Indigenous Women in Guatamala and Mexico," in *Can the Subaltern Speak? Reflections on the History of an Idea*, ed. Rosalind C. Morris (New York: Columbia University Press, 2010), 213–24.

5   Franco, "Moving from Subalternity," 217.

6   Leerom Medovoi, Shakar Raman, and Benjamin Johnson, "Can the Subaltern Vote?," *Socialist Review* 20, no. 3 (1990): 134.

7   Gayatri Chakravorty Spivak, "Terror: A Speech After 9-11," *Boundary 2* 31, no. 2 (2004): 85.

8   Neil Lazarus and Sorcha Gunne, "Mind the Gap: An Interview with Neil Lazarus," *Postcolonial Text* 7, no. 3 (2012): 6.

9   Neil Lazarus, *The Postcolonial Unconscious* (Cambridge: Cambridge University Press, 2011).

10 Aijaz Ahmad, *In Theory: Classes, Nations, Literatures* (London: Verso, 1994).

11 Aijaz Ahmad, "The Politics of Literary Postcoloniality," *Race and Class* 36, no. 3 (1995): 16.

MODULE 12
WHERE NEXT?

KEY POINTS

- Gayatri Chakravorty Spivak's question "Can the Subaltern Speak?" will remain urgent as long as society continues to marginalize subalterns.*

- At first, Spivak's answer to the question she posed seemed to be "No." But over time she came to see education as a way for subalterns to increase their chances of speaking* for themselves. So, in addition to her theoretical project, she has been active in promoting education for the poor.

- Spivak's essay recognizes the complex ways in which subaltern voices are silenced, and equips us with theoretical means to try to overcome this.

Potential

What can Gayatri Chakravorty Spivak's "Can the Subaltern Speak?" offer us today? Her essay asks us to remain skeptical of how the less fortunate are represented, and to be on guard against thinking one can speak in the place of subalterns. As Spivak would agree, her essay presents neither a plan of action nor a clear blueprint for change. Rather, she shows that such grand plans, which claim to give answers that hold true now and forever in any context, can do more harm than good, and must always be questioned. The essay, in its various forms, can be thought of as a draft that requires modification as circumstances change. It is because of this constant process of revision that Spivak's strategies can be adapted to meet the demands of new historical and cultural landscapes.

> 66 The education system in India is in crisis; in rural areas, fewer than one in five poor children of around 11 years of age have even the most basic of literacy and numeracy skills, although most have been in school for five years. 99
>
> Louise Walsh, "Education that Adds Up"

Spivak's examples focus on colonial* and postcolonial* India. But her main idea—that subaltern voices are systematically silenced in political and legal systems, and systems of representation—can be used to analyze other places and times. Thanks to Spivak's essay, we now have a greater understanding of the ways academia, economics, politics, religion, and law work together to mute subaltern voices. Spivak's essay shows how this process of silencing operates, and so implies both that we should help promote subaltern speech, and that we should try to develop a new way of hearing that would allow us to "learn to learn from the subaltern."[1]

Future Directions

Writing in 2010, Spivak noted that "the trajectory of 'Can the Subaltern Speak?' has not yet ended for me."[2] In parallel with her theoretical work, Spivak continues to work as an activist, and remains committed to the ethical project of her earlier work. Of the many future directions in which the core ideas of "Can the Subaltern Speak?" could lead, perhaps the most important is the furthering of education for subalterns. If, in her original 1988 essay, Spivak concluded that the subaltern could not speak, it seems that in the intervening years she has decided that education might offer a way of improving their situation.

Spivak has established schools in India and has taught in rural China and elsewhere. These schools, made possible by her unflagging commitment to education as much as her "dollar salary,"[3] coexist with a national system of education that Spivak claims "makes sure the subaltern will not be heard except as beggars."[4] By working together with subalterns, and listening to them "patiently and carefully,"[5] she hopes to "nurture … the intuition of the public sphere."*[6] That is, she hopes to promote a way of thinking among subalterns that could lead to them representing themselves politically, and so do away with the need to be represented by others.

Summary

"Can the Subaltern Speak?" is the best-known and most controversial work that Spivak has produced. Scholars Sandhya Shetty and Elizabeth Jane Bellamy state the essay is recognized as having a "foundational or canonical status within postcolonial theory."[7] The postcolonial critic Robert Young* goes so far as to name Spivak, along with Edward Said* and the Indian scholar Homi Bhabha* (the author of the influential *The Location of Culture*), the "'Holy Trinity' of postcolonial theory,"[8] and it is in large part this essay that gained her this status.

Why is it that this essay has been so widely discussed, and why does it continue to be read? One answer to these questions lies in the political project of "Can the Subaltern Speak?" That project questions the routine misrepresentation and silencing of subalterns, and exposes the structures of power that lie behind this. Spivak's essay casts a wide net, showing that instances of subaltern silencing must be understood not as isolated cases, but rather as the normal consequence of a world that systematically blocks the voices of the oppressed from being heard. These concerns are as pressing today as they were when Spivak's essay was published, as we face the task of understanding an increasing wealth gap between rich and poor,[9] and when even the right to have one's issues covered by the news media is as often bought as earned.

In "Can the Subaltern Speak?" Spivak refuses to offer any clear solution or propose a course of action that we should take—both the essay's largest failure and its greatest strength. To spend more time discussing one's own methods than actually doing something, and to refuse to commit to a plan of action, might look like a luxury that only academics can afford. What use is continuous questioning about methodology to Bangladeshi peasants trying to feed their children, or to indigenous populations in South America being forced from their land? Further, the deconstructive* project of "Can the Subaltern Speak?" is so thorough that it eventually turns on itself, holding its own methods up for scrutiny. If every method is to be questioned, shouldn't deconstruction itself also be doubted? These are questions worth considering.

Despite these possible shortcomings, Spivak's essay stands as a powerful antidote to intellectual self-satisfaction. Nobody is spared from her process of inquiry, including Spivak herself. "Can the Subaltern Speak?" keeps its importance because the question of its title should continue to be repeated for as long as powerful hierarchies continue to keep subalterns in their place. If we are not willing to create a society in which everyone has a voice, Spivak asks, can we ever be proud of it? Although the question Spivak poses in the title of her essay appears simple, it gets to the very heart of what it means to live in a fair society.

NOTES

1   Stephen Morton, *Gayatri Spivak: Ethics, Subalternity and the Critique of Postcolonial Reason* (Cambridge: Polity, 2007), 160.

2   Gayatri Chakravorty Spivak, "In Response: Looking Back, Looking Forward," in *Can the Subaltern Speak? Reflections on the History of an Idea*, ed. Rosalind C. Morris (New York: Columbia University Press, 2010), 235–6.

3   Spivak, "In Response," 229.

4   Spivak, "In Response," 229.

5   Spivak, "In Response," 232.

6   Spivak, "In Response," 230.

7   Sandhya Shetty and Elizabeth Jane Bellamy, "Postcolonialism's Archive Fever," *Diacritics* 30, no. 1 (2000): 26.

8   Robert J. C. Young, *Colonial Desire: Hybridity in Theory, Culture and Race* (London: Routledge, 1995), 163.

9   Deborah Hardoon, "Wealth: Having It All and Wanting More," Oxfam GB, January 19, 2015, accessed November 27, 2015, http://policy-practice. oxfam.org.uk/publications/wealth-having-it-all-and-wanting-more-338125.

GLOSSARIES

GLOSSARY OF TERMS

Bengal Famine: a 1943 famine in the Indian region of Bengal that led to somewhere between 1.5 and 4 million deaths.

Canon: the ensemble of books, and, in a broader understanding, paintings, music, and other artworks, that have traditionally been understood in the West as the finest to have been produced. The canon came under attack from the 1960s onwards, as critics questioned the criteria—Western, patriarchal, elitist—they claimed it upheld.

Capitalism: an economic system in which the majority of companies and industries are privately owned and run to make a profit for their owners, and in which markets are used to dictate production and decide pricing and income.

Center–Periphery model: a model in which authority is concentrated in a center (the colonizing country), and is only slightly, if at all, influenced by its periphery (the current or former colonies). It implies that the periphery is dependent on the center, but that the inverse is not true.

Colonialism: a system in which one country occupies the territory of another, enforces its own system of governance, and exploits the colonized country economically. In distinction to imperialism, under which a country can hold power over another from a distance, colonialism implies a permanent settlement of colonizers, who hold political allegiance to their home country.

Commonwealth Literature: a field of study that examines literary works from territories that were once part of the British Empire.

Creole: a person descended in full or in part from European colonists. In the context of Spivak's essay it refers to the mixed-race descendants of Europeans and African slaves born in the Caribbean islands.

Critical theory: often used to describe the work of the philosophical school known as the Frankfurt School, "critical theory" is more broadly an approach to social and cultural analysis that incorporates philosophical concerns.

Cultural imperialism: a term indicating what happens when the dominance of industrialized nations determines economic and social progress and cultural values worldwide.

Cultural turn: a movement in the humanities from the early 1970s onwards. In the practice of history, this meant a move from purely political or economic histories, to historical analysis concerned with the way language works, and how cultural artifacts such as objects or novels might also be used to write history.

Deconstruction: a school of philosophy and an analytic approach concerned with revealing the ideological biases that lie behind philosophical and literary concepts and language. Representative figures include the French thinker Jacques Derrida, the Belgian critic Paul de Man, and the American critic J. Hillis Miller.

Discourse: generally, a system of language and assumptions employed to discuss or consider a subject; in the context of poststructural thought, "discourse" refers to the ways in which ideology is expressed through language.

Discourse analysis: a method of analysis, often associated with the work of Michel Foucault, that considers how language and its relation to the social world are influenced by power structures. It might, for example, look at how societally powerful figures use language to confirm their dominant position.

Disinterested: impartial, not influenced by considerations of personal gain. It is not to be confused with "uninterested," meaning "not interested."

Epistemic violence: in Spivak's usage, this refers to the ideology that lies behind Western education and language. She uses the term "violence" since the knowledge produced by the West about others both constitutes a form of violence, to her mind, and has been used to justify real violence against others.

Essentialism: belief that there are natural, essential characteristics of things and people.

Ethnicity: identity based on shared social, cultural, linguistic, or national experience.

Ethnocentrism: belief that one's own ethnicity is superior to that of others.

Eurocentrism: belief that Europe is superior to other parts of the world.

Feminism: thought and practice that advocates for the equality of the sexes in all spheres of society.

Gender: traits distinguishing masculinity from femininity, taking into account social behavior as well as, or instead of, purely biological difference.

Global South: refers to the nations of Africa, Latin America, and most of Asia. It is used in counterpoint with the Global North, meaning the economically dominant parts of the globe, especially Europe and America.

Hegemony: a system in which certain groups exercise power over others. It is often used to describe hierarchies in society.

Hinduism: the practices of certain religious groups, concentrated in India and Nepal. Hinduism is the world's third most popular religion, and is distinctive in that it is more a set of practices than a codified religion, having no prophets, leaders, or set texts.

Ideology: a set of opinions or beliefs, used to understand the world, and in some instances to try to change it. Ideologies are often, but not exclusively, political or religious—capitalist ideology or Christian ideology, for example.

Imperialism: a system in which one nation dominates the political, economic, and cultural life of another. Unlike colonialism it does not necessarily imply the presence of a settled population or administrative and military control by the dominant country.

Indian independence: the moment on August 15, 1947, at which India became independent from British colonial rule. This date marks the culmination of a long history of resistance, dating back to the 1750s, when India first came under British colonial influence through the East India Company.

Intersectionality: a set of theories that make the case for how oppressive institutions (which are racist, sexist, homophobic, classist, and so on) work together and so cannot be examined in isolation.

Jane Eyre: an 1847 novel by the English author Charlotte Brontë, published under the pseudonym Currer Bell. It describes part of the life of protagonist Jane Eyre, during which she comes to adulthood and falls in love.

Literary theory: a body of writing that has been used to read literary texts through philosophical and political frameworks. It can be thought of as the specifically literary manifestation of cultural theory.

Marxism: the ideas, theories and methods of the German political philosopher Karl Marx (1818–83). According to Marxist thought, social conflict caused by economic factors is the driving force behind society's processes and structures.

Metaphysics: a branch of philosophy that sets out to answer fundamental questions about the basic natures of things, and the first principles of understanding.

Modernity: both a historical period and the set of behaviors (rationalism, capitalism, industrialization, urbanization, individualism, and so on) that belong to that period. While its historical span is debated, most agree that it was firmly in place from at least the late 1700s.

Orient: a term traditionally used (although it is now considered insulting by some) to describe countries to the east of Europe, particularly the Middle East and Far East. In postcolonial theory, it is used in opposition to the West.

Other: a term used in philosophy to denote what is distinct from the Self. In postcolonial usage, it refers to those on the periphery in the Center–Periphery model, and is used to imply the marginalization, or exclusion, of the Other.

Padma Bhushan: an Indian award given to civilians who have performed an important service to the nation.

Patriarchy: a system of societal organization in which men hold most or all positions of power, and use this to further the interests of men, usually at the expense of women.

Postcolonialism: a set of approaches used to analyze the global effects of colonialism, particularly through language and culture. Despite the name, postcolonial studies are not restricted to the period following independence, but also analyze the history, culture, politics and economics of countries during colonial rule.

Poststructuralism: the writings of a body of mostly French philosophers such as Jacques Derrida, Michel Foucault, and Gilles Deleuze, who were grouped together during their reception by English-speaking academics in the 1960s and 1970s. It typically calls into question the structures through which knowledge is produced, and so destabilizes claims to universal truth.

Proletariat: a term used by the political philosopher Karl Marx to describe the lowest rank of wage-earners (factory workers, cleaners, etc.) in a capitalist society. In common usage, it often refers to the poorest section of the working class.

Psychoanalysis: a set of psychological theories and techniques created by the Austrian neurologist Sigmund Freud, which suggests that a struggle between unconscious and conscious processes determines human behavior.

Public sphere: the contexts in social life in which social or political issues are discussed. It can be made up of private people gathered together physically as a public to talk through the needs of society, or in a virtual form, such as Twitter.

Relativism: a theory proposing that standards of truth, morality, or any other value judgment are not universal, but rather are valid only for those who hold them.

Revisionism: a process in which accepted beliefs about, for example, history, are reexamined.

Sati: an old Hindu funeral rite in which a wife would commit suicide after her husband's death, often by immolation on his funeral pyre.

September 11 attacks: a series of attacks on the United States, carried out by the terrorist group Al-Qaeda. These included the suicide attacks that brought down New York's World Trade Center.

Speaking: in Spivak's understanding, to speak necessitates being heard. Speaking is a transaction between speaker and listener.

Strategic essentialism: a process in which the knowledge that essentialism is a myth is temporarily suspended to achieve a political goal.

Subaltern: a term that originated in the work of the Italian political philosopher Antonio Gramsci (1891–1937). While its meaning is questioned, in postcolonial studies, subalterns are people subordinated as a result of their class, caste, age, gender or office, or in any other way.

Subaltern Studies Group: also known as the Subaltern Studies Collective, this group of academics focuses on the role of subalterns in South Asian studies. Key figures include Ranajit Guha, Partha Chatterjee, and Shahid Amin.

Third World: a Cold War term that defined the countries that were aligned with neither NATO nor the Communist Bloc. It is now used to talk about countries in the developing world, as Spivak does in her essay, but is considered pejorative by some, as it implies these countries to be inferior.

Universalism: the belief that there are aspects of life and experience that are true regardless of cultural context. In postcolonial theory, this usually implies Eurocentrism, or US-centrism, in which the West imposes its beliefs on other cultures.

West: a term used in postcolonial studies to designate Europe and the United States. It is often used in opposition to "the Orient," "the rest," or non-European countries.

PEOPLE MENTIONED IN THE TEXT

Aijaz Ahmad is an Indian Marxist literary theorist. His books include *In Theory: Classes, Nations, Literatures* (1992) and *In Our Time: Empire, Politics, Culture* (2007).

Simone de Beauvoir (1908–86) was a French existentialist philosopher with a particular interest in ethics and feminism. Her best known work is *The Second Sex* (1949).

Walter Benjamin (1892–1940) was a German thinker whose work, associated with the Frankfurt School, made him a prominent philosopher and cultural critic. Among his many works is the 1936 essay "The Work of Art in the Age of Mechanical Reproduction."

Homi Bhabha (b. 1949) is an Indian-born postcolonial critic who is currently the Anne F. Rothenberg Professor of English and American Literature and Language at Harvard University. He is best known for his book *The Location of Culture* (1994).

Bhuvaneswari Bhaduri: a young woman who hanged herself in 1926 as a way of expressing her unwillingness to carry out a political assassination. Spivak uses her as an example of the impossibility of subaltern speech.

Charlotte Brontë (1816–55) was an English novelist, best known for her works *Jane Eyre* and *Villette*. According to some analyses, her work anticipates more modern feminist concerns.

Judith Butler (b. 1956) is an American academic, specializing in gender theory and philosophy. She is best known for her 1990 book *Gender Trouble: Feminism and the Subversion of Identity*, which argues that gender is performed, rather than intrinsic (an inherent, "natural" property).

Aimé Césaire (1913–2008) was a Martiniquais author, politician, and thinker. He was a left-wing intellectual, a vocal opponent of colonialism, and a proponent of civic engagement.

Partha Chatterjee (b. 1947) is an Indian academic, and founding member of the Subaltern Studies Group. His work is interdisciplinary, with a focus on history and political science.

Kimberlé Crenshaw (b. 1959) is a university professor at the UCLA School of Law. She works primarily on race and the law.

Gilles Deleuze (1925–95) was a French thinker who wrote mainly about philosophy and the arts. In much of his work he argues against the certainty that identity can ever be stable.

Jacques Derrida (1930–2004) was a French Algerian philosopher, best known for his theory of deconstruction, and his radical reinterpretations of the canon of Western philosophy. His best-known work is his 1967 *De la grammatologie* [*Of Grammatology*].

Terry Eagleton (b.1943) is a prominent British literary critic and theorist who was instrumental in introducing literary theory into the study of English literature.

Frantz Fanon (1925–61) was a thinker, psychiatrist, and political radical from Martinique. He is best known for his anti-colonial thinking, and his analysis of the psychological trauma caused by colonialism.

Michel Foucault (1926–84) was a French philosopher, theorist, and literary critic. His work examines the complicity of power and knowledge, particularly in institutions such as the asylum, the clinic, and the jail.

John Gallagher (1919–80) was a British historian who worked at the universities of Oxford and Cambridge. His work focused on the British Empire, including the influential work *Africa and the Victorians: The Official Mind of Imperialism* (1961), which he published with Ronald Robinson.

Mohandas Karamchand Gandhi (1869–1948), also known by the honorific "Mahatma" Gandhi, was an Indian lawyer, and later political activist, who was highly prominent in the Indian independence movement.

Ranajit Guha (b. 1923) is an Indian historian who has worked with the Subaltern Studies Group. He is best known for his book *Elementary Aspects of Peasant Insurgency in Colonial India* (1983).

J. A. Hobson (1858–1940) was a British critic of imperialism, who based his work on economic and historical evidence. He is probably best known for his 1902 work *Imperialism*.

Jacques Lacan (1901–81) was a French psychoanalyst who lectured at the University of Paris VIII. He is known for his controversial theories about the nature of the human psyche, based on poststructuralist rereadings of Sigmund Freud.

John M. MacKenzie (b. 1943) is a British imperial historian, who was based at the University of Lancaster. He is well known for his work on the role of culture in empire, and his best-known work is *Propaganda and Empire* (1984).

Paul de Man (1919–83) was a Belgian-born literary theorist and proponent of deconstruction who worked in America. His collection of essays, *Blindness and Insight* (1971) and his essay "The Resistance to Theory" (1982) are his most famous works.

Karl Marx (1818–83) was a German philosopher and economist whose economic theories provided the foundations of our current understanding of labor's relation to capital. He is best known for his monumental work *Capital* (1867).

Ronald Robinson (1920–99) was a historian of the British Empire, based at Oxford University. Together with John Gallagher, he published the influential work *Africa and the Victorians: The Official Mind of Imperialism* (1961).

Edward Said (1935–2003) was an academic and public intellectual, widely recognized as one of the founders of postcolonial criticism. His seminal book *Orientalism* (1978) examines the misrepresentations of the Orient by the West.

Robert Young (b. 1950) is a British historian and postcolonial theorist, now based at New York University, where he is the Julius Silver Professor of English and Comparative Literature. He is perhaps best known for his book *Colonial Desire: Hybridity in Theory, Culture and Race* (1995).

WORKS CITED

WORKS CITED

Ahmad, Aijaz. *In Theory: Classes, Nations, Literatures*. London: Verso, 1994.

————. "The Politics of Literary Postcoloniality." *Race and Class* 36, no. 3 (1995): 1–20.

Alexander, M. Jacqui, and Chandra Talpade Mohanty, eds. Introduction: Genealogies, Legacies, Movements. In *Feminist Genealogies, Colonial Legacies, Democratic Futures*, xiii–xlii. New York; London: Routledge, 1997.

Ashcroft, Bill, Gareth Griffiths, and Helen Tiffin. *The Empire Writes Back*. London: Routledge, 1989.

———— eds. *The Post-colonial Studies Reader*. London: Taylor & Francis, 1995.

Beauvoir, Simone de. *The Second Sex*. New York: Vintage, 1973.

Butler, Judith. *Bodies that Matter: On the Discursive Limits of "Sex."* New York; London: Routledge, 1993.

————. "Exacting Solidarities." *London Review of Books* 21, no. 13 (1999): 2.

Chatterjee, Partha. "Reflections on 'Can the Subaltern Speak?': Subaltern Studies after Spivak." In *Can the Subaltern Speak? Reflections on the History of an Idea*, edited by Rosalind C. Morris, 81–6. New York: Columbia University Press, 2010.

Cheah, Peng. "Biopower and the New International Division of Reproductive Labour." In *Can the Subaltern Speak? Reflections on the History of an Idea*, edited by Rosalind C. Morris, 179–212. New York: Columbia University Press, 2010.

Eagleton, Terry. "In the Gaudy Supermarket." *London Review of Books* 21, no. 10 (1999): 3–6.

Franco, Jean. "Moving from Subalternity: Indigenous Women in Guatemala and Mexico." In *Can the Subaltern Speak? Reflections on the History of an Idea*, edited by Rosalind C. Morris, 213–24. New York: Columbia University Press, 2010.

Gandhi, Mohandas Karamchand. *Hind Swaraj or Indian Home Rule* [1909]. Ahmedabad: Navajivan, 1938.

Guha, Ranajit. *A Subaltern Studies Reader, 1986–1995*. New Delhi: Oxford University Press, 1997.

Hardoon, Deborah. "Wealth: Having It All and Wanting More." Oxfam GB. January 19, 2015. Accessed November 27, 2015. http://policy-practice.oxfam.org.uk/publications/wealth-having-it-all-and-wanting-more-338125.

Howe, Stephen, ed. *The New Imperial Histories Reader*. London; New York: Routledge, 2009.

Lazarus, Neil. *The Postcolonial Unconscious*. Cambridge: Cambridge University Press, 2011.

Lazarus, Neil, and Sorcha Gunne. "Mind the Gap: An Interview with Neil Lazarus." *Postcolonial Text* 7, no. 3 (2012): 1–15.

Loomba, Ania. "Dead Women Tell No Tales: Issues of Female Subjectivity, Subaltern Agency and Tradition in Colonial and Post-colonial Writings on Widow Immolation in India." *History Workshop*, no. 36 (1993): 209–27.

MacKenzie, John M. *Propaganda and Empire: The Manipulation of British Public Opinion, 1880–1960*. Manchester: Manchester University Press, 1984.

Medovoi, Leerom, Shakar Raman, and Benjamin Johnson. "Can the Subaltern Vote?" *Socialist Review* 20, no. 3 (1990): 133–49.

Morris, Rosalind C., ed. *Can the Subaltern Speak? Reflections on the History of an Idea*. New York: Columbia University Press, 2010.

Morton, Stephen. *Gayatri Spivak: Ethics, Subalternity and the Critique of Postcolonial Reason*. Cambridge: Polity, 2007.

Pandey, Gyanendra, Partha Chatterjee, and Moyukh Chatterjee. "Reflecting on 30 Years of Subaltern Studies: Conversations with Profs. Gyanendra Pandey and Partha Chatterjee." Accessed October 14, 2015. http://www.culanth.org/curated_collections/6-subaltern-studies/discussions/14-reflecting-on-30-years-of-subaltern-studies-conversations-with-profs-gyanendra-pandey-and-partha-chatterjee.

Parry, Benita. "Problems in Current Theories of Colonial Discourse." *Oxford Literary Review* 9, no. 1 (1987): 27–58.

Prakash, Gyan. "Postcolonial Criticism and Indian Historiography." *Social Text*, no. 31/32 (1992): 8–19.

Said, Edward. *Orientalism*. New York: Pantheon, 1978.

Shetty, Sandhya, and Elizabeth Jane Bellamy. "Postcolonialism's Archive Fever." *Diacritics* 30, no. 1 (2000): 25–48.

Spivak, Gayatri Chakravorty. *A Critique of Postcolonial Reason: Toward a History of the Vanishing Present*. Cambridge, MA: Harvard University Press, 1999.

———. "Can the Subaltern Speak?" In *Marxism and the Interpretation of Culture*, 271–313. Basingstoke: Macmillan Education, 1988.

———. *Death of a Discipline*. New York: Columbia University Press, 2003.

———. "Deconstructing Historiography." In *Selected Subaltern Studies*, edited by Ranajit Guha and Gayatri Chakravorty Spivak, 3–32. New Delhi: Oxford University Press, 1988.

———. "Diasporas Old and New: Women in the Transnational World." *Textual Practice* 10, no. 2 (1996): 245–69.

———. "French Feminism in an International Frame." *Yale French Studies*, no. 62 (1981): 154–84.

———. "In Response: Looking Back, Looking Forward." In *Can the Subaltern*

Speak? Reflections on the History of an Idea, edited by Rosalind C. Morris, 227–36. New York: Columbia University Press, 2010.

———. *The Post-colonial Critic: Interviews, Strategies, Dialogues*. Edited by Sarah Harasym. London: Routledge, 1990.

———. "Righting Wrongs." In *Human Rights, Human Wrongs: Oxford Amnesty Lectures 2001*, edited by Nicholas Owen, 164–227. Oxford: Oxford University Press, 2003.

———. "Scattered Speculations on the Subaltern and the Popular." *Postcolonial Studies: Culture, Politics, Economy* 8, no. 4 (2005): 475–86.

———. *The Spivak Reader: Selected Works of Gayati Chakravorty Spivak*. Edited by Donna Landry and Gerald MacLean. New York: Routledge, 1995.

———. "Terror: A Speech after 9-11." *Boundary 2* 31, no. 2 (2004): 81–111.

———. "Three Women's Texts and a Critique of Imperialism." *Critical Inquiry* 12, no. 1 (1985): 243–61.

———. "Translation as Culture." In *In Translation: Reflections, Refractions, Transformations*, edited by Paul St-Pierre and Prafulla C. Kar, 263–76. Amsterdam: John Benjamins, 2007.

Spivak, Gayatri Chakravorty, and Nazish Brohi. "In Conversation with Gayatri Spivak." *Dawn*. Accessed October 15, 2015. http://www.dawn.com/news/1152482.

Spivak, Gayatri Chakravorty, and Elizabeth Gross. "Criticism, Feminism and the Institution: An Interview with Gayatri Chakravorty Spivak." *Thesis Eleven*, no. 10/11 (1984/5): 175–87.

Spivak, Gayatri Chakravorty, and Leon de Kock. "Interview with Gayatri Chakravorty Spivak: New Nation Writers Conference in South Africa." *ARIEL: A Review of International English Literature* 23, no. 3 (1992): 29–47.

Spivak, Gayatri Chakravorty, and Bulan Lahiri. "In Conversation: Speaking to Spivak." *The Hindu*, February 5, 2011. Accessed November 27, 2015. http://www.thehindu.com/books/in-conversation-speaking-to-spivak/article1159208.ece.

Spivak, Gayatri Chakravorty, Sara Danius, and Stefan Jonsson. "An Interview with Gayatri Chakravorty Spivak." *Boundary 2* 20, no. 2 (1993): 24–50.

Vinayaraj, Yahu T. "Spivak, Feminism, and Theology." *Feminist Theology* 22, no. 2 (2014): 144–56.

Young, Robert J. C. *Colonial Desire: Hybridity in Theory, Culture and Race*. London: Routledge, 1995.

———.*Postcolonialism: An Historical Introduction*. Oxford: Blackwell, 2001.

THE MACAT LIBRARY
BY DISCIPLINE

The Macat Library By Discipline

AFRICANA STUDIES

Chinua Achebe's *An Image of Africa: Racism in Conrad's Heart of Darkness*
W. E. B. Du Bois's *The Souls of Black Folk*
Zora Neale Huston's *Characteristics of Negro Expression*
Martin Luther King Jr's *Why We Can't Wait*
Toni Morrison's *Playing in the Dark: Whiteness in the American Literary Imagination*

ANTHROPOLOGY

Arjun Appadurai's *Modernity at Large: Cultural Dimensions of Globalisation*
Philippe Ariès's *Centuries of Childhood*
Franz Boas's *Race, Language and Culture*
Kim Chan & Renée Mauborgne's *Blue Ocean Strategy*
Jared Diamond's *Guns, Germs & Steel: the Fate of Human Societies*
Jared Diamond's *Collapse: How Societies Choose to Fail or Survive*
E. E. Evans-Pritchard's *Witchcraft, Oracles and Magic Among the Azande*
James Ferguson's *The Anti-Politics Machine*
Clifford Geertz's *The Interpretation of Cultures*
David Graeber's *Debt: the First 5000 Years*
Karen Ho's *Liquidated: An Ethnography of Wall Street*
Geert Hofstede's *Culture's Consequences: Comparing Values, Behaviors, Institutes and Organizations across Nations*
Claude Lévi-Strauss's *Structural Anthropology*
Jay Macleod's *Ain't No Makin' It: Aspirations and Attainment in a Low-Income Neighborhood*
Saba Mahmood's *The Politics of Piety: The Islamic Revival and the Feminist Subject*
Marcel Mauss's *The Gift*

BUSINESS

Jean Lave & Etienne Wenger's *Situated Learning*
Theodore Levitt's *Marketing Myopia*
Burton G. Malkiel's *A Random Walk Down Wall Street*
Douglas McGregor's *The Human Side of Enterprise*
Michael Porter's *Competitive Strategy: Creating and Sustaining Superior Performance*
John Kotter's *Leading Change*
C. K. Prahalad & Gary Hamel's *The Core Competence of the Corporation*

CRIMINOLOGY

Michelle Alexander's *The New Jim Crow: Mass Incarceration in the Age of Colorblindness*
Michael R. Gottfredson & Travis Hirschi's *A General Theory of Crime*
Richard Herrnstein & Charles A. Murray's *The Bell Curve: Intelligence and Class Structure in American Life*
Elizabeth Loftus's *Eyewitness Testimony*
Jay Macleod's *Ain't No Makin' It: Aspirations and Attainment in a Low-Income Neighborhood*
Philip Zimbardo's *The Lucifer Effect*

ECONOMICS

Janet Abu-Lughod's *Before European Hegemony*
Ha-Joon Chang's *Kicking Away the Ladder*
David Brion Davis's *The Problem of Slavery in the Age of Revolution*
Milton Friedman's *The Role of Monetary Policy*
Milton Friedman's *Capitalism and Freedom*
David Graeber's *Debt: the First 5000 Years*
Friedrich Hayek's *The Road to Serfdom*
Karen Ho's *Liquidated: An Ethnography of Wall Street*

John Maynard Keynes's *The General Theory of Employment, Interest and Money*
Charles P. Kindleberger's *Manias, Panics and Crashes*
Robert Lucas's *Why Doesn't Capital Flow from Rich to Poor Countries?*
Burton G. Malkiel's *A Random Walk Down Wall Street*
Thomas Robert Malthus's *An Essay on the Principle of Population*
Karl Marx's *Capital*
Thomas Piketty's *Capital in the Twenty-First Century*
Amartya Sen's *Development as Freedom*
Adam Smith's *The Wealth of Nations*
Nassim Nicholas Taleb's *The Black Swan: The Impact of the Highly Improbable*
Amos Tversky's & Daniel Kahneman's *Judgment under Uncertainty: Heuristics and Biases*
Mahbub Ul Haq's *Reflections on Human Development*
Max Weber's *The Protestant Ethic and the Spirit of Capitalism*

FEMINISM AND GENDER STUDIES

Judith Butler's *Gender Trouble*
Simone De Beauvoir's *The Second Sex*
Michel Foucault's *History of Sexuality*
Betty Friedan's *The Feminine Mystique*
Saba Mahmood's *The Politics of Piety: The Islamic Revival and the Feminist Subject*
Joan Wallach Scott's *Gender and the Politics of History*
Mary Wollstonecraft's *A Vindication of the Rights of Woman*
Virginia Woolf's *A Room of One's Own*

GEOGRAPHY

The Brundtland Report's *Our Common Future*
Rachel Carson's *Silent Spring*
Charles Darwin's *On the Origin of Species*
James Ferguson's *The Anti-Politics Machine*
Jane Jacobs's *The Death and Life of Great American Cities*
James Lovelock's *Gaia: A New Look at Life on Earth*
Amartya Sen's *Development as Freedom*
Mathis Wackernagel & William Rees's *Our Ecological Footprint*

HISTORY

Janet Abu-Lughod's *Before European Hegemony*
Benedict Anderson's *Imagined Communities*
Bernard Bailyn's *The Ideological Origins of the American Revolution*
Hanna Batatu's *The Old Social Classes And The Revolutionary Movements Of Iraq*
Christopher Browning's *Ordinary Men: Reserve Police Batallion 101 and the Final Solution in Poland*
Edmund Burke's *Reflections on the Revolution in France*
William Cronon's *Nature's Metropolis: Chicago And The Great West*
Alfred W. Crosby's *The Columbian Exchange*
Hamid Dabashi's *Iran: A People Interrupted*
David Brion Davis's *The Problem of Slavery in the Age of Revolution*
Nathalie Zemon Davis's *The Return of Martin Guerre*
Jared Diamond's *Guns, Germs & Steel: the Fate of Human Societies*
Frank Dikotter's *Mao's Great Famine*
John W Dower's *War Without Mercy: Race And Power In The Pacific War*
W. E. B. Du Bois's *The Souls of Black Folk*
Richard J. Evans's *In Defence of History*
Lucien Febvre's *The Problem of Unbelief in the 16th Century*
Sheila Fitzpatrick's *Everyday Stalinism*

The Macat Library By Discipline

LITERATURE

Chinua Achebe's *An Image of Africa: Racism in Conrad's Heart of Darkness*
Roland Barthes's *Mythologies*
Homi K. Bhabha's *The Location of Culture*
Judith Butler's *Gender Trouble*
Simone De Beauvoir's *The Second Sex*
Ferdinand De Saussure's *Course in General Linguistics*
T. S. Eliot's *The Sacred Wood: Essays on Poetry and Criticism*
Zora Neale Huston's *Characteristics of Negro Expression*
Toni Morrison's *Playing in the Dark: Whiteness in the American Literary Imagination*
Edward Said's *Orientalism*
Gayatri Chakravorty Spivak's *Can the Subaltern Speak?*
Mary Wollstonecraft's *A Vindication of the Rights of Women*
Virginia Woolf's *A Room of One's Own*

PHILOSOPHY

Elizabeth Anscombe's *Modern Moral Philosophy*
Hannah Arendt's *The Human Condition*
Aristotle's *Metaphysics*
Aristotle's *Nicomachean Ethics*
Edmund Gettier's *Is Justified True Belief Knowledge?*
Georg Wilhelm Friedrich Hegel's *Phenomenology of Spirit*
David Hume's *Dialogues Concerning Natural Religion*
David Hume's *The Enquiry for Human Understanding*
Immanuel Kant's *Religion within the Boundaries of Mere Reason*
Immanuel Kant's *Critique of Pure Reason*
Søren Kierkegaard's *The Sickness Unto Death*
Søren Kierkegaard's *Fear and Trembling*
C. S. Lewis's *The Abolition of Man*
Alasdair MacIntyre's *After Virtue*
Marcus Aurelius's *Meditations*
Friedrich Nietzsche's *On the Genealogy of Morality*
Friedrich Nietzsche's *Beyond Good and Evil*
Plato's *Republic*
Plato's *Symposium*
Jean-Jacques Rousseau's *The Social Contract*
Gilbert Ryle's *The Concept of Mind*
Baruch Spinoza's *Ethics*
Sun Tzu's *The Art of War*
Ludwig Wittgenstein's *Philosophical Investigations*

POLITICS

Benedict Anderson's *Imagined Communities*
Aristotle's *Politics*
Bernard Bailyn's *The Ideological Origins of the American Revolution*
Edmund Burke's *Reflections on the Revolution in France*
John C. Calhoun's *A Disquisition on Government*
Ha-Joon Chang's *Kicking Away the Ladder*
Hamid Dabashi's *Iran: A People Interrupted*
Hamid Dabashi's *Theology of Discontent: The Ideological Foundation of the Islamic Revolution in Iran*
Robert Dahl's *Democracy and its Critics*
Robert Dahl's *Who Governs?*
David Brion Davis's *The Problem of Slavery in the Age of Revolution*

The Macat Library By Discipline

Alexis De Tocqueville's *Democracy in America*
James Ferguson's *The Anti-Politics Machine*
Frank Dikotter's *Mao's Great Famine*
Sheila Fitzpatrick's *Everyday Stalinism*
Eric Foner's *Reconstruction: America's Unfinished Revolution, 1863-1877*
Milton Friedman's *Capitalism and Freedom*
Francis Fukuyama's *The End of History and the Last Man*
John Lewis Gaddis's *We Now Know: Rethinking Cold War History*
Ernest Gellner's *Nations and Nationalism*
David Graeber's *Debt: the First 5000 Years*
Antonio Gramsci's *The Prison Notebooks*
Alexander Hamilton, John Jay & James Madison's *The Federalist Papers*
Friedrich Hayek's *The Road to Serfdom*
Christopher Hill's *The World Turned Upside Down*
Thomas Hobbes's *Leviathan*
John A. Hobson's *Imperialism: A Study*
Samuel P. Huntington's *The Clash of Civilizations and the Remaking of World Order*
Tony Judt's *Postwar: A History of Europe Since 1945*
David C. Kang's *China Rising: Peace, Power and Order in East Asia*
Paul Kennedy's *The Rise and Fall of Great Powers*
Robert Keohane's *After Hegemony*
Martin Luther King Jr.'s *Why We Can't Wait*
Henry Kissinger's *World Order: Reflections on the Character of Nations and the Course of History*
John Locke's *Two Treatises of Government*
Niccolò Machiavelli's *The Prince*
Thomas Robert Malthus's *An Essay on the Principle of Population*
Mahmood Mamdani's *Citizen and Subject: Contemporary Africa And The Legacy Of Late Colonialism*
Karl Marx's *Capital*
John Stuart Mill's *On Liberty*
John Stuart Mill's *Utilitarianism*
Hans Morgenthau's *Politics Among Nations*
Thomas Paine's *Common Sense*
Thomas Paine's *Rights of Man*
Thomas Piketty's *Capital in the Twenty-First Century*
Robert D. Putman's *Bowling Alone*
John Rawls's *Theory of Justice*
Jean-Jacques Rousseau's *The Social Contract*
Theda Skocpol's *States and Social Revolutions*
Adam Smith's *The Wealth of Nations*
Sun Tzu's *The Art of War*
Henry David Thoreau's *Civil Disobedience*
Thucydides's *The History of the Peloponnesian War*
Kenneth Waltz's *Theory of International Politics*
Max Weber's *Politics as a Vocation*
Odd Arne Westad's *The Global Cold War: Third World Interventions And The Making Of Our Times*

POSTCOLONIAL STUDIES

Roland Barthes's *Mythologies*
Frantz Fanon's *Black Skin, White Masks*
Homi K. Bhabha's *The Location of Culture*
Gustavo Gutiérrez's *A Theology of Liberation*
Edward Said's *Orientalism*
Gayatri Chakravorty Spivak's *Can the Subaltern Speak?*

PSYCHOLOGY

Gordon Allport's *The Nature of Prejudice*
Alan Baddeley & Graham Hitch's *Aggression: A Social Learning Analysis*
Albert Bandura's *Aggression: A Social Learning Analysis*
Leon Festinger's *A Theory of Cognitive Dissonance*
Sigmund Freud's *The Interpretation of Dreams*
Betty Friedan's *The Feminine Mystique*
Michael R. Gottfredson & Travis Hirschi's *A General Theory of Crime*
Eric Hoffer's *The True Believer: Thoughts on the Nature of Mass Movements*
William James's *Principles of Psychology*
Elizabeth Loftus's *Eyewitness Testimony*
A. H. Maslow's *A Theory of Human Motivation*
Stanley Milgram's *Obedience to Authority*
Steven Pinker's *The Better Angels of Our Nature*
Oliver Sacks's *The Man Who Mistook His Wife For a Hat*
Richard Thaler & Cass Sunstein's *Nudge: Improving Decisions About Health, Wealth and Happiness*
Amos Tversky's *Judgment under Uncertainty: Heuristics and Biases*
Philip Zimbardo's *The Lucifer Effect*

SCIENCE

Rachel Carson's *Silent Spring*
William Cronon's *Nature's Metropolis: Chicago And The Great West*
Alfred W. Crosby's *The Columbian Exchange*
Charles Darwin's *On the Origin of Species*
Richard Dawkin's *The Selfish Gene*
Thomas Kuhn's *The Structure of Scientific Revolutions*
Geoffrey Parker's *Global Crisis: War, Climate Change and Catastrophe in the Seventeenth Century*
Mathis Wackernagel & William Rees's *Our Ecological Footprint*

SOCIOLOGY

Michelle Alexander's *The New Jim Crow: Mass Incarceration in the Age of Colorblindness*
Gordon Allport's *The Nature of Prejudice*
Albert Bandura's *Aggression: A Social Learning Analysis*
Hanna Batatu's *The Old Social Classes And The Revolutionary Movements Of Iraq*
Ha-Joon Chang's *Kicking Away the Ladder*
W. E. B. Du Bois's *The Souls of Black Folk*
Émile Durkheim's *On Suicide*
Frantz Fanon's *Black Skin, White Masks*
Frantz Fanon's *The Wretched of the Earth*
Eric Foner's *Reconstruction: America's Unfinished Revolution, 1863-1877*
Eugene Genovese's *Roll, Jordan, Roll: The World the Slaves Made*
Jack Goldstone's *Revolution and Rebellion in the Early Modern World*
Antonio Gramsci's *The Prison Notebooks*
Richard Herrnstein & Charles A Murray's *The Bell Curve: Intelligence and Class Structure in American Life*
Eric Hoffer's *The True Believer: Thoughts on the Nature of Mass Movements*
Jane Jacobs's *The Death and Life of Great American Cities*
Robert Lucas's *Why Doesn't Capital Flow from Rich to Poor Countries?*
Jay Macleod's *Ain't No Makin' It: Aspirations and Attainment in a Low Income Neighborhood*
Elaine May's *Homeward Bound: American Families in the Cold War Era*
Douglas McGregor's *The Human Side of Enterprise*
C. Wright Mills's *The Sociological Imagination*

The Macat Library By Discipline

Thomas Piketty's *Capital in the Twenty-First Century*
Robert D. Putman's *Bowling Alone*
David Riesman's *The Lonely Crowd: A Study of the Changing American Character*
Edward Said's *Orientalism*
Joan Wallach Scott's *Gender and the Politics of History*
Theda Skocpol's *States and Social Revolutions*
Max Weber's *The Protestant Ethic and the Spirit of Capitalism*

THEOLOGY

Augustine's *Confessions*
Benedict's *Rule of St Benedict*
Gustavo Gutiérrez's *A Theology of Liberation*
Carole Hillenbrand's *The Crusades: Islamic Perspectives*
David Hume's *Dialogues Concerning Natural Religion*
Immanuel Kant's *Religion within the Boundaries of Mere Reason*
Ernst Kantorowicz's *The King's Two Bodies: A Study in Medieval Political Theology*
Søren Kierkegaard's *The Sickness Unto Death*
C. S. Lewis's *The Abolition of Man*
Saba Mahmood's *The Politics of Piety: The Islamic Revival and the Feminist Subject*
Baruch Spinoza's *Ethics*
Keith Thomas's *Religion and the Decline of Magic*

COMING SOON

Chris Argyris's *The Individual and the Organisation*
Seyla Benhabib's *The Rights of Others*
Walter Benjamin's *The Work Of Art in the Age of Mechanical Reproduction*
John Berger's *Ways of Seeing*
Pierre Bourdieu's *Outline of a Theory of Practice*
Mary Douglas's *Purity and Danger*
Roland Dworkin's *Taking Rights Seriously*
James G. March's *Exploration and Exploitation in Organisational Learning*
Ikujiro Nonaka's *A Dynamic Theory of Organizational Knowledge Creation*
Griselda Pollock's *Vision and Difference*
Amartya Sen's *Inequality Re-Examined*
Susan Sontag's *On Photography*
Yasser Tabbaa's *The Transformation of Islamic Art*
Ludwig von Mises's *Theory of Money and Credit*

The Macat Library By Discipline

Macat Disciplines

Access the greatest ideas and thinkers across entire disciplines, including

Postcolonial Studies

Roland Barthes's *Mythologies*
Frantz Fanon's *Black Skin, White Masks*
Homi K. Bhabha's *The Location of Culture*
Gustavo Gutiérrez's *A Theology of Liberation*
Edward Said's *Orientalism*
Gayatri Chakravorty Spivak's *Can the Subaltern Speak?*

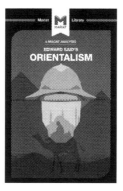

Macat analyses are available from all good bookshops and libraries.

Access hundreds of analyses through one, multimedia tool.
Join free for one month **library.macat.com**

Macat Disciplines

Access the greatest ideas and thinkers across entire disciplines, including

AFRICANA STUDIES

Chinua Achebe's *An Image of Africa: Racism in Conrad's Heart of Darkness*

W. E. B. Du Bois's *The Souls of Black Folk*

Zora Neale Hurston's *Characteristics of Negro Expression*

Martin Luther King Jr.'s *Why We Can't Wait*

Toni Morrison's *Playing in the Dark: Whiteness in the American Literary Imagination*

Macat analyses are available from all good bookshops and libraries.

Access hundreds of analyses through one, multimedia tool. Join free for one month **library.macat.com**

Macat Disciplines

Access the greatest ideas and thinkers across entire disciplines, including

FEMINISM, GENDER AND QUEER STUDIES

Simone De Beauvoir's
The Second Sex

Michel Foucault's
History of Sexuality

Betty Friedan's
The Feminine Mystique

Saba Mahmood's
*The Politics of Piety:
The Islamic Revival and
the Feminist Subject*

Joan Wallach Scott's
*Gender and the
Politics of History*

Mary Wollstonecraft's
*A Vindication of the
Rights of Woman*

Virginia Woolf's
A Room of One's Own

Judith Butler's
Gender Trouble

 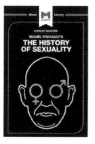  

Macat analyses are available from all good bookshops and libraries.

Access hundreds of analyses through one, multimedia tool.
Join free for one month **library.macat.com**

Macat Disciplines

Access the greatest ideas and thinkers across entire disciplines, including

CRIMINOLOGY

Michelle Alexander's
The New Jim Crow: Mass Incarceration in the Age of Colorblindness

Michael R. Gottfredson & Travis Hirschi's
A General Theory of Crime

Elizabeth Loftus's
Eyewitness Testimony

Richard Herrnstein & Charles A. Murray's
The Bell Curve: Intelligence and Class Structure in American Life

Jay Macleod's
Ain't No Makin' It: Aspirations and Attainment in a Low-Income Neighborhood

Philip Zimbardo's
The Lucifer Effect

Macat analyses are available from all good bookshops and libraries.

Access hundreds of analyses through one, multimedia tool.
Join free for one month **library.macat.com**

Macat Disciplines

Access the greatest ideas and thinkers across entire disciplines, including

INEQUALITY

Ha-Joon Chang's, *Kicking Away the Ladder*

David Graeber's, *Debt: The First 5000 Years*

Robert E. Lucas's, *Why Doesn't Capital Flow from Rich To Poor Countries?*

Thomas Piketty's, *Capital in the Twenty-First Century*

Amartya Sen's, *Inequality Re-Examined*

Mahbub Ul Haq's, *Reflections on Human Development*

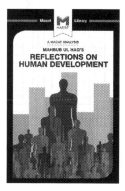

Macat analyses are available from all good bookshops and libraries.

Access hundreds of analyses through one, multimedia tool.
Join free for one month **library.macat.com**

Printed in the United States
by Baker & Taylor Publisher Services